IN THE FOOTSTEPS OF JESUS

In the Footsteps of Jesus

Exploring the World of the Gospels

ROY LENNOX

RESOURCE *Publications* · Eugene, Oregon

IN THE FOOTSTEPS OF JESUS
Exploring the World of the Gospels

Resource Publications
An Imprint of Wipf and Stock Publishers
199 W. 8th Ave., Suite 3
Eugene, OR 97401

www.wipfandstock.com

PAPERBACK ISBN: 978-1-6667-7827-4
HARDCOVER ISBN: 978-1-6667-7828-1
EBOOK ISBN: 978-1-6667-7829-8

VERSION NUMBER 10/30/23

Contents

Palestine in the Time of Herod

○ CITY OR TOWN
■ FORTRESS
┉┉ KINGDOM OF HEROD
⋯⋯ ASHKALON FREE CITY
- - - DECAPOLIS

PROVINCE OF SYRIA

Mt. Lebanon
Mt. Hermon

Sidon
Damascus

Caesara
Philippi

Tyre

GAULANITIS

TRACHONITIS

GALILEE

Bethsaida-
Julias

BATANAEA

Ptolemais

Capernaum

Raphana

The Great
Sea

Sepphoris
Cana
Mt. Carmel
Nazareth
Dora

Sea of
Galilee
Tiberias
Hippos

Dion
AURANITIS

Mt. Tabor
Gadara
Abila

Nain

Caesarea
Maritima

Wadi
Kishon
Mt. Gilboa
Scythopolis
Pella

River Jordan

SAMARIA

DECAPOLIS

Seabaste (Samaria)
Neapolis
Mt. Ebal
Mt. Gerizim

Gerasa

Antipatris

Joppa
Arimathea
Lydda

Alexandrium
Ephraim

River
Jabbok

Philadelphia

Bethel

Emmaus
JUDEA

PEREA

Jericho
Cyprus

Jerusalem
Bethany
Mt. Pisgah

Azotus

Bethlehem
Hyrcania
Mt. Nebo

Ashkelon

Herodium

Gaza

Hebron

Machaerus

IDUMEA

The Salt Sea

River
Arnon

Masada

Beer-sheba
Malatha

Areopolis

NABATAEAN KINGDOM

Brook
Besor

Brook Zered

| 0 | | 30 Miles |
| 0 | | 30 Kilometers |

LUCIDITY INFORMATION DESIGN, LLC

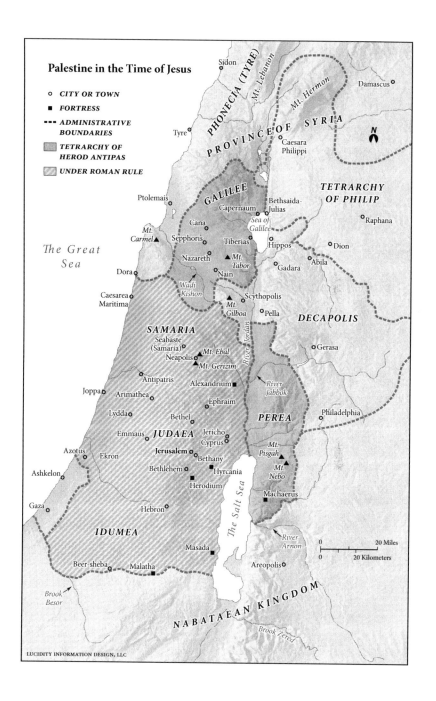

Palestine in the Time of Jesus

- ○ CITY OR TOWN
- ■ FORTRESS
- --- ADMINISTRATIVE BOUNDARIES
- TETRARCHY OF HEROD ANTIPAS
- UNDER ROMAN RULE

Sidon

Damascus

PHONECIA (TYRE)

Mt. Lebanon

Mt. Hermon

Tyre

PROVINCE OF SYRIA

Caesara Philippi

N

TETRARCHY OF PHILIP

Ptolemais

GALILEE

Bethsaida-Julias

Capernaum

Sea of Galilee

Raphana

Cana

Mt. Carmel ▲

Sepphoris

Tiberias

Hippos

Dion

The Great Sea

Nazareth

Mt. Tabor ▲

Gadara

Abila

Dora ○

Nain

Wadi Kishon

Scythopolis

Caesarea Maritima ○

Mt. Gilboa ▲

Pella

DECAPOLIS

SAMARIA

Seabaste (Samaria) ○

Neapolis ○

Mt. Ebal ▲
Mt. Gerizim ▲

Gerasa

River Jordan

Antipatris ■

Alexandrium ■

River Jabbok

Joppa ○

Arimathea ○

Ephraim ○

Philadelphia

Lydda ○

Bethel ○

PEREA

Emmaus ○

JUDAEA

Jericho ○
Cyprus ○

Azotus ○

Jerusalem ○

Ekron ○

Bethany ○

Mt. Pisgah ▲

Ashkelon ○

Bethlehem ○

Hyrcania ■

Mt. Nebo ▲

Herodium ■

Machaerus ■

Gaza ○

Hebron ○

The Salt Sea

IDUMEA

Masada ■

River Arnon

Beer-sheba ○

Malatha ■

Areopolis ○

20 Miles

20 Kilometers

Brook Besor

NABATAEAN KINGDOM

Brook Zered

LUCIDITY INFORMATION DESIGN, LLC

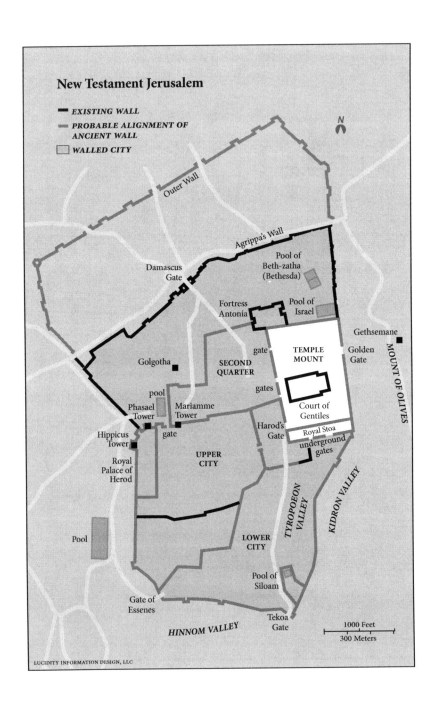

New Testament Jerusalem

- ▬ **EXISTING WALL**
- ▬ **PROBABLE ALIGNMENT OF ANCIENT WALL**
- ▢ **WALLED CITY**

N

Outer Wall

Agrippa's Wall

Damascus Gate

Pool of Beth-zatha (Bethesda)

Fortress Antonia

Pool of Israel

Gethsemane

gate

TEMPLE MOUNT

Golden Gate

MOUNT OF OLIVES

Golgotha

SECOND QUARTER

Court of Gentiles

pool

gates

Phasael Tower

Mariamme Tower

Harod's Gate

Royal Stoa

Hippicus Tower

gate

underground gates

Royal Palace of Herod

UPPER CITY

TYROPOEON VALLEY

KIDRON VALLEY

Pool

LOWER CITY

Pool of Siloam

Gate of Essenes

Tekoa Gate

1000 Feet

300 Meters

HINNOM VALLEY

LUCIDITY INFORMATION DESIGN, LLC

Hasmonaean Dynasty

DATES INDICATE KNOWN DATES OF DEATH

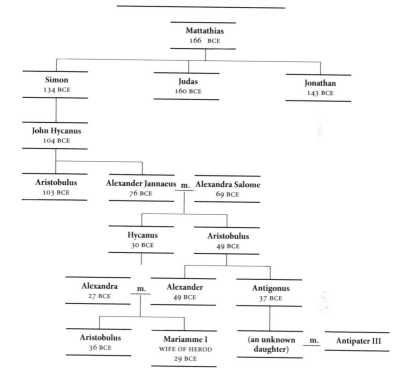

Mattathias
166 BCE

Simon
134 BCE

Judas
160 BCE

Jonathan
143 BCE

John Hycanus
104 BCE

Aristobulus
103 BCE

Alexander Jannaeus m. **Alexandra Salome**
76 BCE   69 BCE

Hycanus
30 BCE

Aristobulus
49 BCE

Alexandra m. **Alexander**
27 BCE   49 BCE

Antigonus
37 BCE

Aristobulus
36 BCE

Mariamme I
WIFE OF HEROD
29 BCE

(an unknown m. **Antipater III**
daughter)

Herod the Great

GOVERNOR OF GALILEE 47 – 41 BCE, TETRARCH OF GALILEE 41 – 40 BCE, KING OF JUDAEA 40/39 BCE – 4 BCE

Doris
FIRST WIFE, WHO HEROD MARRIED IN 47 BCE

Marianne
SECOND WIFE, EXECUTED BY HEROD IN 29 BCE

Marianne II
THIRD WIFE, DIVORCED BY HEROD IN 4 BCE

Malthace
FOURTH WIFE, DIED IN ROME IN 4 BCE

Cleopatra of Jerusalem
LAST WIFE OF HEROD

Antipater II
MARRIED NEICE, MARIAMNE III EXECUTED IN 4 BCE

Alexander
EXECUTED IN 7 BCE

Aristobulus IV
MARRIED COUSIN, BERENICE I EXECUTED IN 7 BCE

Herod II
MARRIED NIECE, HERODIAS, WHO LATER DIVORCED HIM TO MARRY HIS BROTHER ANTIPAS

Archelaus
ETHNARCH OF JUDEA, SAMARIA, & IDUMEA 4 BCE – 6 CE

Antipas
TETRARCH OF GALILEE & PEREA 4 BCE – 39 CE

Philip
TETRARCH OF BATANEA, ITUREA, GAULANITIS, TRACHONITIS, & AURANITIS 4 BCE – 34 CE

Cypros II
MARRIED HER COUSIN ANTIPATER IV

Salampsio
MARRIED HER COUSIN PHASAEL

Olympias
MARRIED COUSIN JOSEPH II, SON OF HEROD'S BROTHER

Berenice I
MARRIED COUSIN ARISTOBULUS IV, 2ND HUSBAND, THEUDON, EXECUTED BY HEROD

Herod V
MARRIED NIECE BERENICE II, THEN COUSIN MARIAMNE V

Tigranes
KING OF ARMENIA 10? – 13? CE

Salome II
DAUGHTER OF HEROD II AND HERODIAS

Cypros III
MARRIED HER COUSIN KING AGRIPPA I

Marianne V
MARRIED HER COUSIN AGRIPPA I

Marianne III
MARRIED HER UNCLE ANTIPATER II

Herodias
WENT INTO EXILE WITH 2ND HUSBAND, ANTIPAS

Agrippa I
"KING HEROD" OF JUDEA 41 – 44 CE

Aristobulus of Chalcis
KING OF CHALCIS 57 – 92 CE

Drusilla
DRUSILLA AND SON DIED IN MT. VESUVIUS ERUPTION

Marianne IV
DAUGHTER OF AGRIPPA I AND HIS COUSIN CYPROS III

Agrippa II
KING OF CHALCIS 49 – 53 CE

Bernice II
QUEEN OF CHALCIS 44 – 81 CE

Introduction

The Lens of History

WHEN I WAS PREPARING to teach a class on the Gospels, I thought it would be easy to find a clear and concise introduction that provided a framework for studying them. One that would not have an axe to grind, either theologically or politically, but rather provide a description of the world that Jesus inhabited. Even though tens of thousands of books have been written about Jesus, the one I was looking for simply did not exist.

There are excellent scholarly books that address this. I have found them to be immensely valuable, but most readers would neither have the time nor inclination to plow through them. Besides that, even though these monographs study different aspects of the subject, not one covers all the issues that I felt needed to be covered. There are many books that focus on Jesus himself, but they do this from a particular theological and sometimes even political point of view, whether as a heavenly king and savior of the world or a political and social revolutionary. No matter how insightful and provocative they might be, I think it's wise to approach the Gospels with an open mind, free of preconceived notions.

My central premise is simple. The more knowledge we have of the world in which the Gospels were written, the better we can understand and interpret them. My aim is not to write a scholarly tome, but rather a book for the general reader based on serious scholarship. At its core this is a personal pilgrimage, a journey through my own education. I invite the reader to take that journey with me, as my companion exploring the world of Jesus.

Even though I've not been trained as a classicist or biblical scholar, I have studied history, receiving a doctorate in it from one of the finest departments in the country. If nothing else, my mentors taught me how to evaluate evidence objectively, without preconceived notions. My later, and much longer, career in financial markets reinforced this; interpretations based on your own biases only breed disaster. And both have taught me that in a world where information is often limited, we need also to trust our intuition if it's based on common sense and unbiased assumptions.

Perhaps my largest audience will be intellectually curious believers, who want to study the Gospels with an open mind from a variety of perspectives. But I hope it will be useful to believers with a more fundamental or evangelical inclination. Perhaps I can persuade them that the complex and even contradictory nature of the Gospels can be viewed as a strength, not a weakness. And finally, non-Christians and unbelievers might also get something out of this, if only that the notion that Jesus never existed is simply nonsensical.

How will I accomplish this? First, we need to understand the political, religious, and social context in which the Gospels were written. Not only is it crucial to recount the Roman conquest and occupation of Jewish Palestine, but it's also essential to grasp the political and social divisions, including endemic economic inequality, in the actual villages and cities where Jesus lived and preached. If the subject of Herod the Great appears to take up inordinate space, it is only because this remarkable, if deeply flawed, man profoundly shaped the society that Jesus inhabited. Herod and his offspring are a recurring, almost haunting, backdrop throughout the narrative of the Gospels.

Likewise, we need to have a grasp of the pagan religions of the Mediterranean world, recounting their vibrant, fluid, and diverse characteristics. Truly this was "a world full of gods," as the esteemed historian Keith Hopkins has termed it. However, we must also examine the religious divisions within Judaism itself. We need to know how the people inhabiting the Gospels lived. What language did they speak? How literate were they? How did they dress? What did they eat? What were their institutions of marriage as well as the conditions and terms of divorce? Finally, the great Jewish revolt and its consequences, namely the sack of Jerusalem and the destruction of the temple, will be recounted, not only for its own sake as an utterly horrible and catastrophic event, but also for its pivotal role in the emergence of Christianity as a new and separate religion as opposed to a minor Jewish cult. The world of Jesus was vibrant and complex; ancient Palestine was an ethnic and cultural cauldron, a more complex world than I originally imagined.

Finally, we need to turn to the Gospels themselves and explore their impact on the growth and development of Christianity. How were they spread? Who read or listened to them? Was there, as one scholar termed it, a "holy internet" that connected the Christian communities in the Roman world? The reader must also be introduced to modern biblical criticism. When were the Gospels written and in what order? Why are Matthew, Mark, and Luke termed the Synoptic Gospels and categorized separately from John? Also, what exactly is the mysterious term "Q" all about? Developed by German biblical scholars in the nineteenth century, it was a catchall term for the sources used by the writers of the Gospels. Were these sources based on some nebulous notion of communal consciousness, as argued by some Biblical critics, or were they reflections of eyewitness testimony? Above all, we must remember that the Gospels are a product of the people of that time, and we are experiencing the story as it unfolds through their eyes not ours. This in no way undermine the Bible's divine inspiration. It is only a reminder that God inspired real people to write the Gospels, ones who possessed their own perspectives and beliefs.

Since the purpose of this book is to provide a framework to approach the Gospels in an informed and analytical manner, I have tried to keep my narrative and analysis as objective and straightforward as possible. When I am provocative, it is not to push a specific agenda or outlook, but rather to encourage the reader to view the subject from different perspectives and be open to new ideas. However, if I do have a thesis, or viewpoint, it is this: The richness and complexity of the Gospels, reflecting the turmoil as well as vibrancy of the world in which they were written, only add to the impact that these texts have on the reader. Even the contradictions between the four Gospel narratives, in my opinion and in that of the early church fathers, do not detract from but rather add to their authenticity. What "authenticity" exactly means depends on the beliefs of the reader, both two thousand years ago and today.

Chapter 1

Rome and Judea

IT IS 63 BCE; Pompey the Great has captured the Temple Mount of Jerusalem after a bloody three-month siege. Rome's greatest general had been busy consolidating the Republic's power in the lands bordering the eastern Mediterranean, when he was invited by one of the two royal brothers from the Hasmonean dynasty of Judea to intercede on his behalf in their struggle for the throne. Despite civil unrest within Jerusalem, it was defended ferociously. The Romans were particularly impressed by the priests of the temple, who faithfully carried out all their ceremonial duties while the battle for the city raged around them. Some were cut down while performing sacrifices as the legionnaires crashed into the temple.

Obviously, this was not an auspicious beginning to the relationship between the Jews and their new masters. To make matters worse, Pompey entered the Holy of Holies after the temple was taken. The Jewish historian Josephus, writing a century and a half later, described the scene. Pompey and his staff entered the sanctuary, the holiest part of the temple, and observed its contents: along with the altar itself, gorgeous lamps, cups of solid gold and rare spices along with two thousand talents of money, a sum worth hundreds of millions of dollars today. Neither he nor his officers laid a finger on anything, and the temple priests were allowed to purify the sacred space the next day, but in Jewish eyes this was sacrilege all the same.

This traumatic event describes Roman relationship with the Jews in a nutshell. Even though the conquerors had no interest in antagonizing their new subjects, extracting wealth and protecting the empire their only priorities, ignorance of the Jews and their unique religion often resulted in insensitive decisions leading to tragic results. However, to fully grasp the nature of Rome's rule of Palestine, we need understand not only how Rome arrived in Judea in the first place, but also the political and social conditions of the land that it conquered.

Rome was originally a small city state in central Italy, built on hills overlooking the river Tiber in the fertile plain of Latium. It rebelled against its petty king and became a republic more than four centuries before Pompey's capture of Jerusalem. Within two hundred years of the Republic's founding, it had conquered the entire Italian peninsula. There were several reasons for Rome's growing dominance, which included its central geographic position ideal for the growth in trade and the projection of military force. However, perhaps the most important reason for the city's political power was its unique constitution. Consisting of a wide franchise of citizens, liberally augmented by immigrants, freed slaves, and citizens from conquered territories, it was governed by a tight-knit network of aristocratic families who controlled the senate and the highest political and military offices. They provided strong political continuity while the rest of the free citizens formed the manpower for the legions. Ultimately it was not Roman law, culture, or any other factor that formed the foundation of Rome's incredible success. It was purely and simply the legions. This brutal, well-disciplined machine would dominate the Mediterranean world for well over half a millennium.

The military term *legion* comes from "legio," or levy of the citizens. Its officers, or tribunes, were recruited from the senatorial and equestrian classes. *Tribune* was derived from the tribe, the largest grouping of Roman citizens. Service as a tribune was essential for political advancement. The title *centurion* was derived from "century," the smallest political segment of the community. Usually from the lower classes, centurions were the backbone of the legions. Often compared to modern non-commissioned officers, they held much more power and prestige, being the equivalent of a company or even a battalion commander today. The army, or legions, therefore, derived their power from the fact that it was an integral component of the Roman body politic.

However, by the time of Pompey the Great, an existential crisis confronted Rome. Could a political system devised for a small, compact city state run an empire? Since the consolidation of Italy, Rome had grown to dominate the entire Mediterranean world. This ascendency started with a life and death struggle with Carthage. Initially a Phoenician trading colony on the North African coast, it would use its immense wealth and sea power to become the dominant imperial power in the western Mediterranean. During the first Punic War, fought from 264 to 242 BCE, the Romans built their own fleet and defeated the Carthaginians on both land and sea, acquiring new colonies: Sicily, Sardinia, and Corsica. Hannibal's invasion of Italy from Spain two decades later forced Rome to fight for its life. Rome eventually drove Hannibal from Italy, defeating the great general outside the walls of Carthage itself, and expelled the Carthaginians from their colonies in the Iberian Peninsula. Finally, in a fit of temper in 146 BCE, Rome besieged Carthage and leveled it to the ground.

The defeat and humiliation of its mortal enemy allowed Rome to set its sights on other targets. However, the conquests of the next two centuries were not systematically planned. Nor were they based, like those of Alexander the Great, on notions of military and personal glory. They were motivated by self-interest and aggrandizement. This allowed Rome to fill the political vacuum formed by the dissolution of the Greek, or Hellenistic, kingdoms formed by Alexander's generals after his untimely death at thirty-two years old in 323 BCE. The first of these wars was against Macedonia, which had been Alexander's homeland, in northern Greece. By 196 BCE, Rome had defeated the Macedonians decisively and acquired political influence over Greece. In 146 BCE, the same year Carthage was destroyed, all of Macedonia and mainland Greece became Roman provinces. The second target, the Seleucid kings, centered in Syria and controlling much of Alexander's Asian Empire, were next. The Romans drove them from Greece, which they were trying to dominate after the Macedonian defeat, and blocked their attempts to invade Egypt. The remainder of the Seleucid Empire in Syria was officially annexed by Pompey shortly before he took Jerusalem.

The republic ultimately proved unsuitable for ruling a large empire. Even while its empire expanded, Rome was torn apart by civil war. Julius Caesar would defeat Pompey but in turn was assassinated in a last gasp of republican resistance. Finally, Caesar's nephew Octavian, the future emperor, Augustus, defeated Marcus Antonius and his consort Cleopatra, queen of Ptolemaic Egypt, at the naval Battle of Actium in 31 BCE. The civil unrest that lasted for almost a century was now replaced by the Pax Romana, or Roman peace. Republican institutions survived in name only. The senate continued to meet, and its members still led the legions and ruled the provinces, but no longer as masters but rather as servants of the emperor. This was the world that Judea and the rest of Jewish Palestine needed to adjust to, a world completely in Rome's orbit.

The experiences of the Jews were quite different; Rome was always the conqueror; the Jews were often the conquered. The Assyrians subjected the northern kingdom of Israel in 722 BCE, shortly after the legendary founding of Rome. Over a century later, in 586 BCE, the Babylonians overran the entire region, including the southern kingdom of Judah. Solomon's Temple in Jerusalem was destroyed and the Judean elite were carried off to Babylon, not to return for fifty years. By the time of the founding of the Roman Republic, the Jews were ruled by the Persians, who had overthrown the Babylonians. Alexander the Great conquered the Persian Empire before his death in 323 BCE. The Jews had the geographic misfortune to lie between Seleucid Syria and Ptolemaic Egypt, who struggled over Palestine for a hundred years, When the Seleucids gained final control in 196 BCE, the story gets extremely interesting.

Unlike the previous conquerors of the Jews, the Greek ruling classes in the Hellenistic kingdoms had a specific agenda, namely cultural assimilation. They aimed to impose every aspect of Greek culture on their subjects. This included not only language, religion, philosophy, and literature but also athletics, theater, and other alien practices. Hellenization represented cultural imperialism to the populations of the non-Greek peoples in the Near East and Egypt. The rural population, with their traditional customs and beliefs, resisted it. However, the urban elites, the people on the make, embraced Hellenism, leading to cultural tension within the broader society. This conflict over Hellenism reflected divisions between the elites and the common people, the city and the country. Nowhere did this play out more dramatically than in Judea, the land of the Jews. This was not surprising. If segments of other ancient cultures were inclined to resist, the provocation for the Jews would be exponential in comparison. Religion was the catalyst.

Pagan religions were anthropomorphic. The gods each identified specific characteristics, including fertility, the wind, wisdom, war, and others. These were easily interchangeable with the gods of other peoples, easing the process of cultural assimilation. Judaism, however, had evolved into a uniquely monotheistic construct, very different from other religions of the ancient world. This fundamental uniqueness represented a ticking time bomb, poised to explode. When it did, civil war and revolt erupted.

In the previous centuries, Judaism had evolved from a syncretic religion marked by alien influences and internal disputes on how to worship God to a strictly monotheistic one regulated by the law, based on the Torah, and centered on the rebuilt temple in Jerusalem. Hellenism, however, represented an existential threat to Judaism, especially after Antiochus IV Epiphanes came to the throne in 174 BCE. The high priest at the time, Onias III, was a traditionalist, but his brother Joshua was the leader of the Hellenizing party, preferring to be called by the Greek form of his name, Jason. He persuaded Antiochus to appoint him as high priest in his brother's place. This was a direct challenge to traditional Jews, the faithful or "Hasidim." The sight of temple priests practicing in the nude at the gymnasium particularly galled them. Tensions grew and civil war broke out in Jerusalem. The Seleucid king reacted violently, even abolishing Jewish laws related to the Sabbath and circumcision. The final insult was the installation of a pagan altar, where sacrifices were made to Zeus, in the temple itself.

Revolt broke out in the rural areas. It was led by the five sons of a priest named Mattathias of the Hasmon family who lived in the hills of northern Judea near the border with Samaria. The oldest son, Judas, nicknamed Maccabee, meaning "the hammer," led the revolt and recaptured the temple and purified it, the inspiration for the festival of Hanukkah. Nevertheless, the war against Antiochus and his successors continued, ebbing and flowing for two decades. It was as much an internal struggle between Jewish factions as a revolt against a foreign occupation. The Maccabees would ultimately prevail due to their clever manipulation of the various contenders for the Seleucid throne, who gave the family the office of high priest in return for political support. Many Jews saw the Maccabees as national liberators, but they would never achieve full legitimacy in the eyes of all their subjects.

Judas, as well as his brother Jonathan, were killed in battle. Finally, Simon, the family's political mastermind, was declared in 140 BCE as both high priest and king, in all but name, finally legitimizing the rule of what was to be known as the Hasmonean dynasty. He would drive the Seleucid forces from the citadel of Jerusalem in 141 BCE. However, he was murdered while in a drunken stupor, but the palace coup failed. John Hyrcanus, his last surviving son, took the throne.

John Hyrcanus ruled for thirty years, consolidating and expanding Hasmonean rule. The internal divisions of the Seleucids left a vacuum in southern Syria that Hyrcanus filled, making his kingdom a major player in the region. He moved north from Jerusalem and destroyed the city of

Samaria, incorporating the surrounding area into his realm. He turned south and not only conquered the Idumeans, or Edomites, ancient enemies of the Jews, but also forcibly circumcised and converted them. His son Judas, better known by his Greek name Aristobulus, succeeded in 104 BCE and ruled for only a year before his death. Nevertheless, he subdued Galilee and forced the native Itureans to convert. They would soon become, as one historian put it, "more Jewish than the Jews," but his people's recent conversion would also taint Jesus when he preached in Judea and Jerusalem. "Nothing good comes from Galilee" became a popular insult.

Aristobulus's younger brother, Alexander Jannaeus, succeeded him and ruled for almost three decades. He continued the aggressive policies of his predecessors; the kingdom would be constantly at war. He subdued the old Philistine cities along the Mediterranean coast, a few settlements on the Sea of Galilee, and the area to the east of it. Across the Jordan, Perea was annexed, and its population converted. This was where John the Baptist would preach and later be executed. A pattern is evident; rural Semite populations were forced to covert, while urbanized Hellenized ones were not. The conversions, most importantly in Galilee and the eastern section of Idumea, were made easier because circumcision was also prevalent in many of these Semitic regions.

The Hasmoneans became the dominant force in the region. The Itureans controlled the north, around modern Lebanon, and the Nabateans, centered around Petra, dominated what is now southern Jordan, but the Jewish state was certainly the strongest. At home, Alexander continued the policy of his father, John Hyrcanus, and supported the Sadducees, who represented the Hellenistic aristocratic party. The Pharisees resented the Hasmonean usurpation of the high priesthood, which was traditionally restricted to the lineage of Aaron. Therefore, despite the expansion of the Hasmonean kingdom, the tensions between Hellenized and devout Jews still existed, as they would up to the great revolt against Rome a century and a half later.

On one hand, the Hasmoneans presented themselves as preservers of ancient Jewish traditions, cloaking themselves in the high priesthood and even using archaic Hebrew on their coinage to connect them to David and the kings of his line. On the other, they acted like Hellenistic monarchs, both diplomatically and militarily, increasingly depending on mercenaries like the states around them. These Hellenistic influences can also be seen in court protocol and the use of Greek names and symbols on coinage. This multicultural and multiethnic land was complex and filled with contradictions. Moreover, it had been and would remain disorderly. Peace and stability required a firm and indeed brutal hand. The idea that social and political instability at the time of Jesus was in some way an anomaly, or what the noted theologian, N. T. Wright, calls a "perfect storm," is simply ludicrous.

Therefore, the Hasmoneans acted and even perceived themselves as Hellenistic kings struggling for regional hegemony, while they maintained an aura of militant Judaism that included forcible conversion, a form of ethnic cleansing of the neighboring rural populations. It was a balancing act: assimilation into the culture of the eastern Mediterranean while maintaining a national Jewish identity. Alexander Jannaeus represented a paradox himself. He pushed the dynasty to the height of its power and was the first of his line to formally call himself king. However, he had a strong temper and a propensity for violence that offended many of his subjects, driving them into rebellion. It was becoming more and more apparent that the descendants of the Maccabees had betrayed the values of their original constituency. This is encapsulated in an account by Josephus. The king celebrated his defeat of the invading Seleucid king Demetrius by crucifying eight hundred rebels from the Pharisee faction in front of their families. An exaggeration by Josephus perhaps, but it vividly captures the persona of Alexander Jannaeus, a man who would use a hated, alien form of execution to terrorize his subjects.

On his death in 76 BCE, he had the wisdom to appoint his wife Salome Alexandra ruler, a woman noted for her piety who had support from the general population. She quelled internal unrest by allying herself with the Pharisees, while doubling the size of the army, maintaining a strong mercenary force to secure the borders. However, her death nine years later left the nation in an untenable situation. Her elder son, Hyrcanus, was the legitimate heir and she appointed him high priest, but he was weak and indecisive. His younger brother, Aristobulus, inherited his father's vices but not his personal strength and military acumen. Civil strife was the result. The door was open for Pompey. The Hasmoneans no longer had the luxury of a weak and divided power to the north.

The incorporation of Pompey's eastern conquests into its empire greatly increased the wealth and power of Rome. At the same time, it was administratively an unwelcome distraction, especially when Rome became embroiled in two decades of civil war. Direct rule was a necessity in Northern Syria. A Roman governor in Antioch commanded the legions necessary to keep the Parthian Empire at bay. On the other hand, the location of the Hasmonean kingdom was not so strategic. Client kings were a more viable option. This opened the door to an ambitious family of recently converted Idumean Jews.

Antipater, a second-generation Jew and the father of Herod the Great, came from one of the leading families of Idumea, which was in what is now southern Israel. The family lived in its capital, Maresha, located just south of Jerusalem in the Judean hills. The eastern part of the kingdom, ancient Edom, was ethnically Arab, circumcised, and closely related culturally to the Jews. Western Idumea bordered the Mediterranean in what was once the ancient land of the Philistines. Hellenized and uncircumcised, it was the original home of Antipater's forefathers.

Antipater was extremely rich. The family's wealth was based not only on extensive flocks of livestock and rich agricultural lands but also on its control of the caravan routes that connected Petra, the capital of the Nabatean Arabs, to the ports on the coast. He solidified his relationship with the Nabateans by marrying Cyprus, a daughter of one of their leading families. Antipater's father had been appointed governor of Idumea by King Alexander Jannaeus. He would follow in his footsteps. Clever, resourceful, eloquent, and ruthless, he was just the sort of adventurer who could thrive in a fluid and anarchic environment. Antipater allied himself with Hyrcanus against his brother Aristobulus. Hyrcanus was the rightful king and was supported by the Pharisees, but he was also weak and ineffectual. Not a bad thing from Antipater's perspective; he could influence and control him.

However, Aristobulus easily defeated his brother outside of Jericho. He promised to spare Hyrcanus's life if he acquiesced to an honorable, if secondary, role. Hyrcanus was inclined to accept the terms, but Antipater convinced him that his brother would not allow him, as the legitimate heir, to survive since he would always be a rallying point for the Pharisees and their supporters. He persuaded him to flee to Petra to gain support from the Nabatean king. Using his wife's family connections, bribery, and the promise to restore Nabatean lands annexed by the Hasmoneans, Antipater persuaded the king to intervene. It was not to be. When the Nabateans reached Jerusalem, they found that Pompey had beat them to it.

Perhaps Antipater's greatest quality was hardheaded realism. It became immediately apparent to him that the road to power now passed through Rome. You left Rome out of the equation at your own deadly risk. For the next two decades Antipater would be a virtuoso at juggling local politics and dancing to the tune of whoever was ascendent in Rome. While continuing to pull the strings for Hyrcanus against his brother, Antipater always remained loyal to Rome, whose interest he served above all others. Neither his royal patron, who ultimately was dethroned, nor the Hasmonean kingdom, which had lost much of its territory, stood a chance against the hand that fed him. Nevertheless, his support of Pompey against Julius Caesar in the civil war nearly led to disaster.

After his crushing defeat by Caesar at Pharsalus in 48 BCE, Pompey fled to Egypt, only to be assassinated on his arrival. Caesar arrived shortly thereafter, only to become involved in a dispute between the young Ptolemaic king and his rebellious older sister Cleopatra. Things at first went badly. Caesar found himself besieged in Alexandria's royal palace. This provided Antipater with a golden opportunity to redeem himself. He raised a force of three thousand Judean soldiers and rushed to Egypt, carrying a message from Hyrcanus, still the high priest, instructing the Jews living in Egypt to support Caesar. This helped to turn the tide, raising the siege and gaining the gratitude of Caesar. Not only did he reward Antipater with Roman citizenship, but he also recognized him as the official administrator of Judea. Even though he was forced to change sides again after Caesar's assassination in 44 BCE, Antipater solidified his power and added back some of the lands that Pompey had removed from Judean jurisdiction. Undoubtedly, he was starting to have dynastic aspirations, even though most Judeans did not consider him, nor later his son Herod, to be a "real Jew." This viewpoint didn't only reflect ethnic prejudice. Whatever issues the Hasmoneans might have had, including the fact that they were not from the line of David, no one could question their Jewish bona fides. As a member of a people forcibly converted only recently, Antipater was highly suspect.

Whether Antipater would have succeeded in his ambition to become king will never be known. His career was cut short by assassination. Antipater was intensely ambitious, a total realist, and undeniably able. However, as one historian has noted, he was also much more merciful than most of his contemporaries. This in part was a reason for his untimely death. He persuaded the Roman governor of Syria to spare one of his local enemies from execution, a fellow Idumean named Malichos. Whether this action was motivated by his natural clemency or the insistence of Hyrcanus is immaterial. Malichos returned the favor by arranging the poisoning of Antipater's wine. His son Herod would never make the same mistake.

Chapter 2

Herod the Great

THE DEATH OF ANTIPATER set the stage for his son Herod. If one were to mention his name today, most people would identify him as the monster in the Gospel of Matthew who ordered "the massacre of the innocents" after he learned of the birth of Jesus in Bethlehem from the Magi. This story is almost certainly false. Although it's conceivable that Jesus could have been born before Herod's death in 4 BCE, the episode is not repeated in the other Gospels or any other source. Interestingly, the Talmud also characterized Herod more as legend than a historical character. Nevertheless, such fantastical stories possess a kernel of truth. They reflect the psyche of the man and the perceptions of those writing about him. He most likely didn't murder the innocents, but if the situation arose, he would not have flinched.

Rather than give credence to legend, it is much more productive to focus on the real man, for the world of Jesus was molded by Herod's larger-than-life personality. Herod could be viewed as the last and perhaps the greatest of the Hasmonean line. Like them he was the quintessential Hellenistic monarch, but one who projected his Jewishness to maintain the loyalty, or at least the grudging acquiescences, of his subjects. Besides this, Herod also had to contend with his patron Rome, a task at which he was remarkably adept.

Almost all we know of Herod the Great comes from the Judeo-Roman historian Josephus, who wrote almost a century after his death, both in *The War of the Jews* and the *Antiquities of the Jews*. On one level this is a blessing. We know more about him than we do of almost any figure in ancient history and certainly any Roman client king. On another level, we need to be very careful. Josephus came from an aristocratic priestly family, who would not have looked kindly on an Idumean-Arab interloper.

Herod first appeared on the scene at the age of twenty-five in 47 BCE. He was the second of the five children of Antipater and his Nabatean Arab wife, Cyprus. His father, at his height of power and influence in the court of Hyrcanus, appointed his older son Phasael governor of Jerusalem and put Herod in charge of Galilee. This proved to be no easy task. The ethnic Iturean population that inhabited the region were fierce and unruly and had only recently been forcibly converted to Judaism. It was no surprise, therefore, that his priority was the pacification of the region, which was plagued by brigandage. Herod moved decisively against one of the most ruthless outlaw bands. He quickly suppressed it and executed the leader, Hezekiah, and all his men. Certainly, a dramatic entrance on the stage of history, but one with serious ramifications.

This decisive act immediately augmented Herod's reputation. The population of the areas bordering Galilee certainly welcomed it. Bandit raids significantly decreased. The governor of Syria, a relative of Julius Caesar, was pleased since it helped him keep the peace in his province. The rich merchants of Jerusalem supported any actions that facilitated commerce and trade. However, the actual population of Galilee itself would not be as supportive. The brigands were their neighbors and kinsmen. Moreover, Herod's actions could be manipulated at court and used against his father Antipater.

Josephus reports that powerful figures at court, including Hyrcanus the king, took exception. The ostensible reason was that Herod did not have the authority to carry out executions of Jews without the permission of the Sanhedrin, or ruling council. This is problematic for two reasons. First, Josephus was anachronistically projecting the authority of this institution back from his time to Herod's. And second, it's doubtful that the governor of Galilee didn't have jurisdiction in cases such as this, especially since it concerned, at least on the surface, public order and common criminals. There must have been other factors driving the demand that Herod journey to Jerusalem and face trial. Court intrigue certainly played a part. There was deep resentment against Antipater, who as an Idumean was perceived as a foreigner. However, there was even more going on.

Brigandage in Jewish Palestine exhibited religious, and often political, characteristics in addition to simple theft and murder. This was true before the time of Herod—even the Maccabees began their resistance as brigands before raising traditional armies—and it would continue after him. In fact, brigandage was endemic in Jewish Palestine. What else would explain the popularity of Barabbas, who the mob demanded to be freed instead of Jesus before his crucifixion? Outlaws and social rebels were one and the same in ancient Judea and Galilee, the Robin Hoods of the ancient world. Not surprisingly, once Herod established himself as king, he would be more proficient at controlling this problem than either his predecessors or successors.

The ruling class of Judea, both Sadducees and Pharisees, grudgingly accepted the reality of Roman domination, but they deeply resented the rule of Antipater and his sons. An argument that Herod exceeded his authority provided an opening. Hezekiah and his followers also had a popular support—the mothers of the executed men maintained a daily vigil, wailing outside the temple—and it became clear that it was an opportune time for a political attack. Antipater realized the gravity of the situation and understood his own vulnerability. He advised Herod to appear at the trial but instructed him to bring bodyguards, not so large a number that could seem intimidating but powerful enough to protect him if the trial went badly. The members of the council conducting the trial were initially intimidated, but one of the Pharisees encouraged them to reach a guilty verdict. At this point, Herod used the ace up his sleeve, a strongly worded letter from the governor of Syria, Sextus Caesar, instructing Hyrcanus to acquit him. Not surprisingly, the weak figurehead lost his nerve and adjourned the trial, begging Herod to leave Jerusalem as quickly as possible. If anything, this potential crisis increased Herod's authority. Sextus Caesar added the city of Samaria and Coele Syria (the Beqaa Valley in modern Lebanon) to his dominions in Galilee. Herod wanted to invade Judea in revenge for his ill treatment. His father and brother wisely advised restraint.

There are several factors at play here. First is the normal court intrigue of a Hellenistic kingdom. A key element of this is the resentment of the few remaining Hasmoneans and their followers against foreign interlopers, who ironically were much better at the game than they were. Second, the brigandage of Hezekiah and his fellow outlaws underlines the social unrest endemic to the society. Third, the political force of Rome is clearly apparent: Herod is the client and Sextus Caesar the patron. Finally, Herod's ruthlessness, decisiveness, and intelligence are all on display in this narrative; but the story is also a harbinger of the challenges ahead of him. He would need to adopt the trappings of a Hellenistic monarch, while simultaneously projecting as much as possible a Jewish identity and maintaining the good will of his Roman patrons. Juggling these different personas was by no means an easy task, but he would become a master of it.

Herod survived and prospered from his first major experience on the political stage. The regions under his control had increased, and he possessed the full confidence of his father and the Roman governor of Syria. After the assassination of Julius Caesar in 44 BC, however, the playing field changed. Showing his usual political dexterity, Antipater quickly changed sides and supported the republicans after Cassius, one of the ringleaders in the assassination, took control of Syria with a large army. Cassius immediately demanded the colossal sum of six hundred talents from Judea. Antipater divided the sum into six parts and delegated the collection to local magnates, including Herod in Galilee. Raising this money was a thankless task. Some areas defaulted. Cassius reacted by selling the populations of four towns into slavery. Antipater personally bailed out his political opponent and future assassin Malichos, the head of another prominent aristocratic Idumean family. For his part, Herod displayed his usual competency, swiftly raising his allocation. This ruthless efficiency further secured his position, but his world was turned upside down by the murder of his father.

Herod's first inclination was to use his forces in Galilee to attack Jerusalem and exact revenge on his father's assassin. However, his brother urged caution, suggesting a meeting with Cassius, who already mistrusted Malichos for his lack of enthusiasm in raising taxes. The Roman governor acknowledged Herod's "debt of honor" and green lighted the murder of Malichos. Herod set up a meeting with his father's assassin on neutral territory, the beach outside the walls of Tyre, and cut him down there. Hyrcanus had accompanied Malichos but swiftly changed sides. With his enemy removed and the support of the king, Herod moved decisively. He crushed a rebellion in Judea led by the assassin's brothers. Then he repelled an invasion from the north by the Iturean king in support of Antigonus, the son of the deceased pretender Aristobulus. On Herod's victorious return to Jerusalem, Hyrcanus rewarded him with the hand of his granddaughter Mariamne in marriage, providing Herod with a strong dose of Hasmonean legitimacy. Already having an Idumean wife was only a minor technicality; monogamy was reserved for the common people, not a potential ruler. His road to power seemed assured.

Any illusions Herod had of peace and security were shattered by the defeat of the assassins of Caesar at the Battle of Philippi. With his patron

Cassius dead, Herod needed to take a page from his father's book. He changed sides . . . and quickly. The victor, Marcus Antonius, was making his way to the east. Herod intercepted him in Bithynia, situated in present day Turkey. Using all his natural charm, Herod reminded the victorious general not only of his late father's loyalty to Caesar but also of the lavish hospitality that Antipater had showed Antony years before when he had visited Jerusalem as a young military tribune. To seal the deal, he showered the Roman with extravagant bribes. Duly impressed, Antony appointed Herod and his brother Phasael tetrarchs, or rulers, of Judea and Galilee respectively. He also freed the Jews who had been sold into slavery by Cassius and further showed favor by adding territory to Judea. Thus, the brothers attached themselves to a new patron, at that point the most powerful man in Rome.

Herod did not have the opportunity to rest on his laurels. The ongoing political instability in Rome left a power vacuum in the border regions of the eastern Mediterranean. This led to power struggles in the region that would take on a distinct *Game of Thrones* flavor. Even Josephus, never a fan of Herod, could not help but show grudging respect when he recounts his maneuvers. It all started in 40 BCE, a year after Herod's official recognition by Antony.

Mattathias Antigonus was one of the last surviving Hasmonean claimants to the throne. He took refuge in the court of Lysanius, king of Iturea. The Itureans, who inhabited the area north and west of Galilee, were a fierce and warlike people, highly valued as mercenaries for their skill as archers. Antigonus had his eyes on Jerusalem and was soon presented with a golden opportunity. Taking advantage of continued unrest in Rome and the vacuum left by Cassius's removal of his legions from Syria, the Parthians invaded.

They presented a formidable threat to the region. A little over a decade before, the Roman general Crassus had invaded Parthia to match the military glories of his colleagues Pompey and Caesar. The Parthians, lethal desert warriors, decimated his army and killed him. Only the quick thinking and decisive action of his second in command, Cassius no less, saved the remnants of his army and blocked an invasion of Syria. The Parthians relished the defeat of Crassus, one of the most powerful men in Rome and surely the richest. One ancient source relates that the Parthians sarcastically poured molten gold down the throat of his corpse while another describes his head being used as a prop during a court performance of a Greek tragedy.

Antigonus persuaded the Parthians to support him against Herod. He promised them one thousand talents, an extraordinary sum, along with a gift of five hundred maidens to be selected from the families of his Jewish enemies. It was agreed that Antigonus would invade Judea independently. The Parthians would only then be asked to mediate at the crucial moment. The rebel prince raised an army in Galilee, some of the recruits likely from the remnants of Hezekiah's followers. Leveraging the element of surprise, Antigonus moved quickly to take Jerusalem. The fighting in the city was vicious, ebbing and flowing through the streets and even enveloping the temple. Phasael defended the royal palace. He succeeded in driving some of Antigonus's forces back, and Herod in turn trapped them in the temple, leaving a contingent of his men surrounding it, but the enemy ambushed and butchered them. An outraged Herod proceed to slaughter not only his foes but also many inhabitants of the city. Bloody hand to hand combat between small bands raged throughout the narrow, crooked streets and alleys of Jerusalem. To make matters worse, the feast of Pentecost was beginning and streams of people from the countryside were entering the city to celebrate. Most of them supported Antigonus, the true Hasmonean, not an Idumean interloper. Herod and Phasael attacked them ferociously, driving some out of the city and others into the temple. At this point Antigonus, well-rehearsed, asked for a truce and suggested Parthian mediation. The fighting subsided; the intrigue commenced.

The Parthian envoy entered the city with a bodyguard of five hundred elite calvary. He was an aristocrat named Pacorus, cupbearer to the king no less. Smooth and persuasive, he suggested a meeting with the local Parthian satrap in Syria. Herod, deeply suspicious, would have none of it, but his brother Phasael and Hyrcanus agreed to negotiate. At first, they were treated respectfully and showered with rich gifts, but Phasael's suspicions became aroused. It was obvious they were being spied upon. He also began to hear rumors of bribery and the shocking offer of a gift of Jewish women to the foreigners. Weighing his limited options and probably cursing his own stupidity, Phasael confronted the satrap, berated him for his duplicity, and offered him more for his freedom than Antigonus had for his crown. Denials and sweet words followed, but the satrap quickly allowed Antigonus to kidnap Phasael and Hyrcanus. Phasael couldn't face the prospect of humiliation. Lacking a dagger or sword he dashed his head against the stone wall of his cell. As the blood oozed from his cracked skull, he whispered in his final breath that he rejoiced that Herod lived for he would surely exact

IN THE FOOTSTEPS OF JESUS

revenge. For his part, Hyrcanus cravenly accepted humiliation. While he was begging for mercy on his knees, Antigonus mutilated his uncle's ears by tearing them out with his own teeth, creating a deformity that ensured that Hyrcanus could never serve as high priest again.

Before word of these events reached Jerusalem, Pacorus sent an upbeat message to Herod, suggesting a meeting. Alexandra, the Hasmonean mother of his betrothed Mariamne, displaying the healthy paranoia embedded in her royal DNA, advised caution. Her counsel, along with unsettling rumors about the treatment of Hyrcanus and his brother, provoked Herod to act. He slipped his family along with a strong contingent of loyal soldiers out of the city in the middle of the night. Herod fled south to his home base in Idumea, depositing his family in the impregnable fortress of Masada. After disbanding most of his army, Herod proceeded to Petra, hoping to summon aid from the Nabatean king. The king, however, ordered him to leave his domain, explaining he was following instructions from the Parthians. Herod was incensed that his ally treated him so. He suspected that this appalling lack of hospitality had nothing to do with a Parthian threat, but rather was related to the large debts that Nabatean merchants owed his family. Forced to change plans, Herod headed west to Alexandria where Cleopatra welcomed him warmly, hoping to entice him to fight for her as a mercenary. Herod had other ideas. He made one of the boldest decisions of his life. Braving the rough, midwinter seas, Herod sailed to Italy.

Herod's objective was straightforward: convince the Romans to aid him in the recovery of Judea from Antigonus. He wanted to be named regent with the teenaged grandson of Hyrcanus, and younger sibling of his wife Mariamne, placed on the throne. The outcome was better than Herod could have hoped for. On his arrival in Rome, Antony introduced him to his fellow triumvir Octavian, on whom Herod, helped along by the usual bribes, made a strong impression. Both men sponsored him before the senate, which confirmed him not as regent but rather as king. Herod's timing was impeccable; the Romans required a strong leader, not a boy, in Judea to stabilize the region. They could not care less that Herod was considered at home as a "half Jew," not even qualified to serve as high priest; he was strong, dependable, and loyal to Rome. That was all that mattered. As Herod left the Senate House with Antony and Octavian walking on either side of him, surrounded by the ruling consuls and the political elite of Rome, he must have seen this as the culmination of his family's hopes and ambitions. Moreover, the title of king and the legitimacy that it bestowed removed any ambiguity about his right to rule. Herod had one problem though: He was a king without a kingdom. His enemies needed to be driven out and obliterated. Ostensibly he had Roman support, but as usual the bulk of the efforts would rest on his shoulders.

Herod arrived in Palestine in the spring of 39 BCE. The Romans had already driven the Parthians from Syria, but Judea was firmly in the hands of Antigonus. Immediately upon landing, Herod hired mercenaries and raised troops from his supporters in Galilee. He moved down the coast to Idumea, raising the siege of Masada, where he had left his family. Support from the Roman forces in Judea was suspiciously lackadaisical, suggesting bribery from Antigonus. Unable to take Jerusalem, Herod concentrated on putting down insurrections in the countryside, especially Galilee where banditry broke out again in that chronically unstable territory. There were numerous caves in the cliff sides that provided refuge to the insurgents. Herod rooted them out cave by cave, lowering his troops in wooden cages down the side of the cliff by ropes. His men used long poles with hooks to pull out the defenders from the mouths of the caves, and flaming projectiles were cast into the interiors. Then they would storm in to finish off the survivors.

Herod still didn't possess the troops necessary to take Jerusalem and end the war. Learning that Antony was fighting in the north, besieging a city on the Euphrates, Herod took a large portion of his troops and rushed to meet with him. At Antioch he learned that the siege was not going well and made a difficult march to assist Antony. The triumvir was so appreciative of Herod's unsolicited assistance that, once the city was taken, he designated the bulk of his army, led by one of his senior commanders, to move south in support. Herod didn't wait for the whole force. With one Roman legion under his sole command and a contingent of Iturean mercenaries, he prepared a lightning thrust south, only to hear the horrifying news that his brother Joseph had been killed in battle, his head chopped off and body mutilated. Incensed, Herod rushed quickly into Galilee. The fighting there, and later in Samaria, was fierce and bloody. Herod threw himself personally into the fray and at one point was pierced in his side by a javelin. The historian Josephus relates that his many close calls gained him the reputation as "darling of heaven." After subjecting the north, he drove toward Jerusalem, meeting the general who had defeated and killed his brother at a small village twenty miles north of the city. Herod obliterated the enemy and forced them into the village, massacring them in ferocious house to house combat. Antigonus's general Pappus fell in the battle and met the same fate he had bestowed on Herod's brother.

Joined by Roman reinforcements, Herod pressed on to Jerusalem. His forces were overwhelming now, with eleven legions and thirty thousand of his own men. Nevertheless, the resistance was fierce both inside and outside the walls, where guerrilla forces harassed foraging parties. A harbinger of the great siege a century later perhaps, but with a major difference. He was a Jew and knew that if he were to assume the crown later, he could not totally antagonize his subjects. When the outer and inner walls fell, he did not disrupt the supply of sacrificial beasts to the temple, which remained in enemy hands. When the temple was finally taken, Herod deployed his own troops to prevent the Romans from pillaging it. And as the Romans began to kill and loot indiscriminately, he implored the Roman commander to restrain his men, asking him if the Romans wished him "to be king of a desert." Sosius refused, arguing the legionnaires could not be refused their customary and time-honored rights after a difficult siege. Herod didn't argue; rather he paid each Roman soldier off out of his own pocket, saving Jerusalem from destruction.

The goal now for Herod was to consolidate the power he had won with cunning, sweat, and blood. Although he saved Jerusalem, Herod had no qualms about liquidating Antigonus's supporters, which included most of the old aristocracy, resulting in the virtual extermination of the royal council. Beyond this, Herod needed to establish his legitimacy as king of Judea through his marriage into the Hasmonean line. At the core, however, his power depended on his role as a client king for Rome. Total loyalty to his patron, Mark Antony, ruler of the East, was paramount. Nevertheless, Herod needed to counter the desire of Antony's consort Cleopatra to add both Palestine and the Arab Nabatean kingdom to her domains. He used all his charm and political savvy to counter her efforts, and Antony's trust of his client ultimately trumped the charms of his lover. Luck also played a role. Herod was not summoned to join Antony and Cleopatra in the Battle of Actium in 31 BCE, where they were decisively defeated by Octavian. At Cleopatra's behest he was waging war against the Nabateans.

Much like his father after Caesar's defeat of Pompey, Herod faced a quandary; he had backed the wrong horse. And like his father, he acted quickly and boldly. He executed the former Hasmonean king Hyrcanus, who he and his father had served loyally for years. This removed a possible contender from the royal line. Herod further secured his position by putting his younger brother in charge at home. He scattered his family among his strongest fortresses, taking care to separate his own relatives from those of his Hasmonean princess's, whose younger siblings were effectively held hostage by his own sister Salome. His home base secure, he proceeded uninvited to the island of Rhodes where Octavian was staying after his conquest of Egypt. Herod was completely honest. He didn't excuse his loyalty to Antony, but assured Octavian he would receive the same devotion. A massive bribe sealed the deal, even resulting in a larger kingdom and the right to choose his own successors. In retrospect, Octavian's acquiescence makes perfect sense. The Jews were not easy to rule. They resented, even hated Rome. The region was politically unstable and susceptible to brigandage. If that were not bad enough, the strange religion of the Jews was hard for an outsider to comprehend, making them prickly and easily insulted. In short, the Jews were just the kind of people client kings were made for and Herod was the ideal candidate. He was cruel and efficient, a Jew himself, and, most importantly, loyal to Rome. Octavian, soon to be Augustus, the first emperor of Rome, never regretted his decision. Herod, on his part, would not only create the world that Jesus would inhabit but also dominate every aspect of it, even the Gospels themselves.

If the "murder of the innocents" surely never happened but reflected an insight into Herod's psyche, his outlandish depiction in the Babylonian Talmud resonates even more. Let's paraphrase the story in that source.

> Herod was a slave in the Hasmonean household. He lusted over a princess of that royal family. Marriage was impossible unless he rebelled. A voice, probably divine, whispered in his mind that the time was right. He slaughtered the entire family apart from the princess. To save herself from marriage, she ran to the roof of the palace and shouted that she was jumping to her death to deny any legitimacy to the usurper. After the princess's suicide, Herod preserved her body in honey for seven years. Some claimed he had sex with it, proving his perversion, while others said it was a bizarre trophy bolstering his fledging legitimacy. This was not the end of his transgressions. Herod also killed the religious sages, who he believed saw him as a non-Jew and foreigner, which precluded him from the throne. He blinded the wisest of them, Bava ben Buta, and tried to trick him into cursing him as an illegitimate king, thus sealing his fate. Admitting his mistake after witnessing the loyalty of the sage, Herod asked him how he could gain atonement. The reply was to rebuild the temple. The temple represented one way to bring light to the world, the Torah the other. As for the

Romans, the wise man said not to worry. They would be angry but would not undo what had been already done.

Certainly a fantastic tale, and a lurid one at that. It is almost dream-like, feverishly delving into the subconscious in order to reflect external reality. Herod certainly wasn't a slave; he came from a prominent Idumean noble family. Nevertheless, his family, for all its power and influence, were in fact servants to the Hasmoneans, without a thread of royal legitimacy. And he did wish to marry a Hasmonean princess, Mariamne, granddaughter to both Hyrcanus and Aristobulus. Unlike the character in the story from the Talmud, however, he did in fact marry her. Yet the story was on the mark in two important ways. Herod was not only madly in love with Mariamne; he also was responsible for her death. Moreover, it completely captures Herod's motivation in building the temple, namely, to accentuate his Jewishness and buttress his legitimacy as king. In short, this tale from the Babylonian Talmud encapsulates the challenges facing Herod and the forces driving his rule.

Herod's relationship with Mariamne was ludicrously operatic. She was cold and manipulative and looked down on her husband and his family, who she saw as Idumean lowlifes. Herod loved Mariamne obsessively, but his love reeked of insecurity and emotional immaturity with a large dose of sexual jealousy mixed in. Mariamne's mother, Alexandra, served as a role model for her daughter. A quintessential royal snob, cunning and ruthless, she had no reservations against plotting against her own son-in-law.

It came to a head in 36 BCE, five years before the defeat of Antony and Cleopatra. The office of high priest was vacant. Traditionally the Hasmonean king served in that office, but Herod did not have the pedigree to even dare fill the position himself, so he chose a Babylonian Jewish non-entity loyal to him alone. Alexandra was incensed; her teenage son Aristobulus, Mariamne's younger brother, was surely the rightful high priest in her eyes. She appealed to Cleopatra who, as we noted earlier, had her own designs on Judea. Herod was forced to give in, but he had serious reservations. Aristobulus was young and handsome and a Hasmonean to boot, potentially a rival for the throne. Despite his obsessive love for his wife, and his fear of Cleopatra's wrath, Herod could not allow this to happen. He invited the entire family to his palace in Jericho and gave a feast in honor of his brother-in-law. After dinner the men retreated to the baths, where the drunken Aristobulus, helped along by Herod's Celtic bodyguards, "accidentally" drowned.

Royal courts by nature are psychological hothouses, the political maneuvers and the personal conflicts inevitably leading to conflicts as intense as any in psychiatric wards. Actions that seem cruel and absurd in normal life take on a logic of their own in this environment. And the infighting in the court of Herod was exacerbated by the pride and jealousy of each of the merged families. Alexandra resented that her princess daughter needed to marry a foreign usurper of questionable Jewishness. Herod's younger sister Salome, for her part, was totally loyal to her brother and hated the pretense and social condescension of her royal in-laws. Suspicion and distrust only increased; matters could only get worse.

Not only did Mariamne spew her invective openly at her husband, but she also made no secret of her disdain for his mother and sister. Salome did everything possible to play on Herod's jealousy, even accusing her sister-in-law of infidelity. Josephus tells us that Salome told her brother that his wife had seductively sent her self-portrait, in effect an ancient "selfie," to Mark Antony, a man with a well-earned reputation of sexual licentiousness. Such insinuations incited Herod's jealousy and increased his insecurity. So, when he was summoned by Mark Antony to explain the death of Aristobulus, Herod was in a terrible psychological state. He ordered Salome's husband, Joseph, to kill Mariamne if he didn't return alive. Antony, however, had no intention of removing his loyal ally over such a minor infraction, even at the expense of upsetting Cleopatra. As usual Herod landed on his feet. Things at home however, got only worse.

Mariamne wheedled the truth out of Joseph. Her own husband had been prepared to murder her if things went badly in Alexandria. When Herod returned home, his wife rejected his sexual advances, declaring she knew the truth. To make matters worse, Herod's sister Salome hinted that her husband, Joseph, had an affair with Mariamne while her brother was gone. Herod was enraged and threatened to kill both his wife and brother-in-law. After calming down—there wasn't a thread of evidence—Herod spared his wife but summarily executed Joseph. Perhaps Salome lost the first round, but her cold-hearted gambit, costing the life of her own husband, speaks both to her own ruthlessness and the level of the stakes. Herod's sexual jealousy and his own insecurity never abated. Yes, he had allowed his queen to live, but in a figurative sense he was simply preserving her body in the vat of honey so vividly evoked in the Talmud. As in any good opera, the tragic ending was inevitable.

A few years later, when Herod journeyed to Rhodes after Antony's defeat at Actium to beg for Octavian's favor, he again left orders for his wife to be killed if he didn't return. As a further precaution to ensure good behavior, he separated Mariamne's children from her as hostages. Shortly after his return, in 29 BCE, Herod and his wife became embroiled in a violent argument. She reprimanded him violently for the murders of her grandfather and brother. As if on cue, Salome directed Herod's cup bearer to approach and accuse Mariamne of planning to poison him with a love potion. Then the queen's chief eunuch was tortured and confessed that his mistress truly hated her husband. Herod tried his wife for treason before his council. Seeing the writing on the wall, Alexandra saved her own skin by turning on her own daughter. For his part, Herod suffered a mental breakdown after the inevitable execution, even calling for his wife, believing her still alive. While he was incapacitated, Alexandra attempted a coup in Jerusalem, but Herod's commanders stayed loyal. This revived him. Alexandra followed her daughter to the grave.

What does this *Game of Thrones*-like soap opera tell us? Why spend so much space recounting the lurid details? The answer is simple: It captures the man and his personality. The story from the Talmud brilliantly captured the psyche of Herod the Great. He was an extremely competent man with charisma to spare, but also a narcissist, a person with deep personal insecurities combined with an extreme sense of entitlement. He couldn't imagine a world where the woman he obsessively loved could survive after his own death. Herod is a man seeking status and legitimacy, loving his wife who personifies those traits, while resenting the condescension that she displays toward him. He's also paranoid, often in the positive way that kept ancient rulers alive, but on the personal level, he allowed it to drive him past the realm of reason. In many respects the internal conflict within his family represented a microcosm of the land he ruled, a multicultural caldron always ready to explode at the least provocation. Ironically, Herod was more adept at maintaining peace in his kingdom than in his own family. Finally, he was perceived by his subjects as larger-than-life, fundamentally influencing the world that Jesus inhabited.

Herod was a strong ruler for a few reasons: intelligence, boldness and ruthlessness, but perhaps most important was his loyalty to Rome and his ability to please and manipulate his patrons. The quintessential outsider, he played off his Jewish subjects, who questioned his authenticity, against his gentile ones, who distrusted his Jewishness. How Herod navigated these waters was the key to survival. Ironically, the Talmud tale hints at a grudging respect for Herod; if not, why would the voice of God urge him to rebel? It also confirms the importance of Rome in the equation, and it provides the key to his attempt to attain Jewish authenticity: the magnificent rebuilding of the Second Temple. The foundation of Herod's rule was supported by a tripod consisting of the three roles he needed to play: client and friend of Rome, Hellenistic ruler, and king of the Jews. Each of these relationships needs to be examined.

The patron-client relationship was the cornerstone of Roman society. No rich senator would ever embark on official business if he were not accompanied by an entourage of clients. The patron in turn provided support to his clients. It could be anything from sponsoring one of them for political office or helping another to gain appointment as a tribune in the legions. A client, on his part, owed his patron complete loyalty. He was expected to pay homage to his patron daily and do his bidding. Political support was a given and social respect a requirement. It was not a monetary relationship but rather a deeply personal one that greased the entire social fabric from top to bottom. Even a freed slave remained the client of his former master, owing loyalty and expecting favors. Even the gang bosses of the Roman underworld sought patronage from the most powerful politicians. Although they operated at a more rarified level of violence, client kings followed the same rules, but their patron was none other than the emperor.

Herod the Great, and his descendants, understood this relationship implicitly. No matter what their loyalties were, whether they were religious, ethnic, or family ones, the first and most important one was to Rome. Doubtless Herod paid bribes to Antony, Octavian, and other powerful Romans at critical moments, but at its heart the arrangement wasn't a financial one. Indeed, Herod would not be required to pay tribute or taxes to Rome. Instead, he was expected to keep the peace at home, protect his own borders, and provide military support to Rome when requested. Despite the size of its empire and the strength of its legions, Rome had limited resources to police and protect its vast domain. The legions of Syria were stationed there as a defense against the Parthians, not to occupy Palestine. A local ruler like Herod was more effective in controlling their own people, especially unruly and rebellious ones. It's not surprising that when serious revolt did break out in 66 CE, it originated in Judea, the area directly controlled by Rome at that time and not in one of the client kingdoms of Herod's successors.

It is a testimony to Herod's abilities that the Romans added to his core territory, making his kingdom as large as, if not a larger, than that of the Hasmoneans at its greatest extent. One example vividly illustrates this phenomenon. Augustus had appointed a man named Zenodorus as tetrarch, or ruler, of the Transjordan region northeast of Herod's kingdom. However, Zenodorus augmented his revenues by allowing brigands in the rugged Trachonitis region to attack the trade routes leading to the wealthy city of Damascus in exchange for a cut of the loot. In 23 BCE, the citizens of Damascus sent a delegation to Rome to complain. Augustus responded by transferring the sovereignty of Trachonitis and the surrounding area, including Gaulanitis, or the Golon Heights, to Herod, deeming the rough terrain as unsuitable for the operations of Roman legions. It was a good deal for both sides. The Romans were able to protect the valuable trade routes without the headache of putting down the brigands themselves. Herod handled the headache, a task he could not refuse, but received substantial new territories, gentile ones in fact, along with the fertile agricultural land bordering it.

In order to perform his obligations to Rome, and to provide personal security, Herod maintained a small but highly proficient professional army commanded by Roman officers recruited from retired centurions. Early in his reign, the bulk of his army was Jewish, but except for Idumeans and some Babylonian Jews, he preferred to recruit from gentiles as he consolidated his power, preferring troops whose prime loyalty was to him alone. The core of his army came from the hellenized city of Samaria, which had always been loyal. In honor of Augustus, he renamed it Sebaste and colonized it with six thousand retired non-Jewish veterans. Herod further supplemented this force with mercenaries from Thrace, Gaul, and even Germany.

However, it was the royal fortresses that formed the spinal cord of his kingdom. Jerusalem was critical. Always an unruly city, especially during the high holy days when it was inundated with hundreds of thousands of pilgrims, it required constant attention. The key to Jerusalem's defense since the days of the Hasmoneans was the citadel contiguous to the temple. Herod strengthened it and refurbished the interior so it could also be used as a palace. He renamed it the "Antonia" in honor of his patron at the time, Mark Antony. He also improved the fortifications of the northwest corner of the city walls by building three massive towers. Finding the proximity of the Antonia too close for comfort to the temple to serve as his residence,

Herod constructed a lavish palace connecting the three towers. These two structures, the new palace and the Antonia, were the backbone of Jerusalem's defenses and served as strategic points to quell unrest within the city.

There were also strong hilltop fortresses throughout the kingdom, some from the Hasmonean period and others newly constructed. The most famous of these fortresses, Masada, was situated on an impregnable one-thousand-foot-high rock plateau in the southern Judean desert near the Dead Sea. It contained lavish royal apartments available in times of crisis. The hellenized city of Sebaste was also provided with new fortifications, which controlled not only Samaria but also the whole central portion of the kingdom. It was also the center of the imperial cult dedicated to Augustus, which for obvious reasons could not be situated in Jerusalem. Other colonies of veterans were established in secure frontier regions, including Galilee and the surrounding Iturean region.

If Herod's role as a client of Rome was secured by political and military force, his persona as a Hellenistic monarch was purely cultural, reflecting a more subtle form of power. Not all his gentile subjects were hellenized, especially in the harsh terrain of the northeast border area, but most of the urban areas, even to some extent Jerusalem but especially along the coast, were culturally Greek. The Greeks were at their core a theatrical people, having invented the medium itself. They totally grasped the importance of playing a role and performing it well. The Hellenistic monarch, for his part, was expected to do the same. The essential purpose of the monarch's performance was to underscore his legitimacy. Specifically, this entailed transmitting to his audience that he was a king favored by the gods and not a "tyrant" forcibly imposed on his subjects.

All royal theater begins with the court, and the court of Herod, with certain modifications to appease his Jewish subjects, was at its core a Hellenistic one. Whereas the languages of the old Hasmonean court included Hebrew and Aramaic as well as Greek, only Greek was spoken in Herod's. His garments reinforced his regal bearing; purple robes and a royal diadem stood out prominently. The diadem was particularly symbolic. It appeared in place of a portrait, prohibited by Jewish custom, on many of Herod's coins, reinforcing the necessity to keep any celebration of a royal cult subtle in a Jewish kingdom. Furthermore, both the court and the central bureaucracy reflected the norms of the Hellenistic East. At the center were Herod's advisors, called *philoi*, "friends" in Greek. His closest friend was a Greek, Eurycles of Sparta. His advisers were almost all hellenized gentiles, whose loyalty was to him alone. One of the most important of these was Nicolaus of Damascus, a renowned scholar and biographer of Herod. This work has unfortunately been lost but was a key source of Josephus's account. Nicolaus served as a companion, advisor, and tutor in the Greek classics to the king.

Perhaps the most dramatic way for Herod to make his mark as a great Hellenistic monarch was to build palaces, fortresses, and most importantly cities and towns. From the time of Alexander the Great, it was simply what a great king did; there was no better way to advertise your political power and beneficence to your subjects. The rebuilding and renaming of the city of Samaria was a prime example of this. An even better one was the construction of Caesarea on the Mediterranean coast. It was destined to be the administrative capital of Judea under Rome and possessed the largest artificial harbor in the Mediterranean world. Although it would house a large Jewish minority, it was planned as a Roman and Hellenistic city with all the accoutrements: temples, forum, gymnasia, theater, and even an amphitheater. Whereas its name honored the emperor, other projects, in the tradition of Hellenistic rulers, he named after himself or members of his family. Herod built the strategically important city of Antipatris on the route between Jerusalem and Caesarea. Phasaelis was constructed in the rich agricultural region of the Jordan valley in honor of his older brother who had died in the hands of the Parthians. It became an important center of the date industry, which produced substantial revenues for the kingdom. He named one of the three great towers in Jerusalem after a friend, but the other two were named after Phasaelis and his wife Mariamne. One of his most impressive projects, a great palace a few miles south of Jerusalem, he named Herodion. It was built on the spot where he defeated a force, ironically a Jewish one, as he fled the capital during the Parthian siege, commemorating both his own survival and the victory of his dynasty. On a clear day it could be seen from Jerusalem and would ultimately become the site of his tomb.

However, there was another way for a Hellenistic monarch to display his wealth and advertise his kingly virtue: bestowing generous patronage to persons or entities that ostensibly were not directly tied to the royal patron. By providing lavish gifts, for instance, to Greek cities throughout the eastern Mediterranean, Herod increased his prestige for the very reason that his generosity was not a quid pro quo arrangement. Such acts of generosity profoundly elevated his status, suggesting that only a man of immense wealth and prestige could show such unencumbered largess.

Herod's philanthropic activities were not only clustered in the Levant but also extended to Hellenistic cities in Asia Minor, the Aegean, and the Greek mainland itself. The building projects he financed included gymnasia, porticos and colonnades, theaters, temples, pavement of streets, port facilities, and even aqueducts. Herod also provided financial endowments to cities, sometimes even aiding the payment of taxes to Rome. Perhaps his greatest coup was a magnificent gift to help finance the Olympic Games. The organizers honored Herod by naming him manager of the games for the rest of his life.

Generosity alone was not the sole catalyst of this royal philanthropy. There were other more pragmatic motives; prestige is only worth so much. Gaining good will had important economic and political benefits as well. For example, Ascalon, located a few miles north of Gaza, was a free city of Idumean ethnicity. It had traditionally supported Herod's family, but it was also an economically vital port on the Mediterranean. Generous support of public building projects made both financial and political sense. Ascalon played a vital role in the commerce of the area, and this directly impacted the wealth of Herod and his realm. Herod often aimed his generosity at entities that were of special importance to Rome, his imperial patron. Antioch was the capital of the province of Syria, the bulwark against the Parthians. Rhodes had been a loyal ally to Rome for many years and the city of Nikopolis held a special place in Emperor Augustus's heart. It was founded to commemorate his victory nearby over Antony and Cleopatra at the Battle of Actium. The gift to it not only honored the emperor; it was also a subtle apology from Herod for backing the wrong horse. Finally, most of the localities benefiting from Herod's largesse also had substantial Jewish populations. In effect he was killing two birds with one stone. Such acts of generosity burnished his reputation with diaspora Jews outside his kingdom and also gained him prestige at home.

However, being a loyal patron of Rome and playing the role of an ideal Hellenistic sovereign were not sufficient. Herod also needed to project himself unequivocally as a Jewish king, in the mold of David, Solomon, and even his Hasmonean predecessors. As a "half Jew," this was not an easy task, but keeping the most significant segment of his population quiet was of critical importance. Until recently, most historians accepted Josephus's view that Herod lacked Jewish authenticity, pretending cynically to be one solely for political purposes. Current research, however, suggests a different interpretation in respect to Herod's authenticity. In fact, Herod considered himself a Jew above everything else and led a distinctively Jewish life. As the historian Adam Marshak puts it: "He was not a Hellenized monarch who simply happened to be born a Jew . . . he was a fully Hellenistic, Romanized Jewish king." Although this seems at first to be a rather subtle distinction, it is a fundamental one.

One way to establish this point is to look at the coinage that was minted during Herod's reign. Except for two minor and ambiguous exceptions, he faithfully obeyed the prohibitions in Exodus of portraying graven images or likenesses of living things. Another is to look at the decoration and architecture of his palaces. Not only are the beautiful mosaics almost always adorned with geometric, not figurative, shapes, but the baths are designed for both routine and ritualized bathing. Herod's policy toward marriage indicates that he took his Jewish identity seriously. Out of his ten wives (although uncommon in normal society, polygamy was not prohibited by Jewish law at that time), five unambiguously were Jewish and the others converted. The women of his family were required to marry Jews. When the Nabatean suitor of Herod's beloved sister Salome refused to be circumcised, the betrothal was annulled. In addition, archeological excavations of the kitchens of Herodian palaces suggest that the food prepared followed the dietary laws. A famous quote of the emperor Augustus reinforces this conclusion. He quipped that he "would rather be Herod's pig than his son." The first part of the quote is obvious. The second will become so.

However, leading a relatively pious life was not enough for a man who wanted to be the king of the Jews within his realm and the patron to all those living outside. Copying only the Hasmoneans to gain legitimacy would not assuage the man's enormous ego. He needed to be another David, a new Solomon, the progenitor of a revived golden age. The way to accomplish this was to create a new, more prestigious Jerusalem and rebuild the temple, at that time a poor replica of Solomon's, and make it the epicenter of Jewish life, gathering all twelve tribes of Israel, a "house for all nations." Perhaps it wasn't only ego. On a deeper psychological level he felt profound guilt for many of his actions, most notably the judicial murder of his beloved wife. Indeed, as the sage Bava Ben Buta suggested in the Babylonian Talmud, rebuilding the temple was a way for Herod to gain atonement.

The rebuilding of the Second Temple by Herod resulted in the creation of one of the most significant architectural achievements of the time. The construction started around 20 BCE, after Herod had consolidated his power. Most of it was completed by his death, but work continued on and off until 64 CE, when the release of thousands of workers at its final completion added to the unrest leading to the great revolt. The new, rebuilt temple, by providing employment and attracting visitors from all over the Mediterranean world, drove the economy of the city, which in turn benefited all of Judea.

The inspiration for the building itself came from the scriptures. First Kings provides a detailed physical description of Solomon's Temple, which included specific measurements. Furthermore, the prophet Ezekiel, who lived at the time of the destruction of the First Temple and the Babylonian exile, related a vision that described in detail its replacement. This very detail constrained innovation in respect to the sanctuary. Its measurements and decorative garnishes were precisely defined. The altar was to be made of fieldstone untouched by iron and faced east. Access would be from the old City of David from the south. Any architectural innovation, therefore, needed to be confined to the public areas, and Herod took full advantage of all the possibilities.

Already, during the Hellenistic period of Jerusalem, a public space, or agora, surrounded the sanctuary. This served to bind together the sacred and political life of the city. The new temple would be built on a commanding height, comparable to the Acropolis of Athens, but with the agora situated on the mount rather than lying at its base. Indeed, Greek influences on Herod's Temple were readily apparent. Mathematical symmetry was a key component, as was the case of Greek temples like the Parthenon. It utilized the Greek practice of *entasis* in the design of the Corinthian columns surrounding public spaces. They were slightly concave to allow them to hold greater weight and evoke an illusion of linear perfection.

Roman influence also played a paramount role in Herod's Temple. This was not surprising; Rome was his patron and he was personally familiar with the city, having visited it twice. This influence is apparent in the sheer magnitude of the project. He doubled the size of the Temple Mount, which had already dominated the city, to thirty-five acres, making it the largest sanctuary site in the ancient world. This required shifting vast amounts of earth and building not only enormous retaining walls but also constructing arches and vaults more than a hundred feet below the surface to support the platform.

Herod created what was in effect a Roman forum surrounding the sanctuary. A double colonnaded portico, sixty feet wide and forty feet high, enveloped these public plazas. The columns were marble and the roof beams cedar. The total combined length of the portico was three thousand and nine hundred feet. Following the custom of the time, portions of the portico displayed the wealth of the sovereign, especially spoils of war. This vast space surrounded by porticos was Jerusalem's primary public meeting place. Business was transacted there, much like it was in the Roman forum. One can also imagine religious teachers lecturing under the porticos and tourists from all over the ancient world milling about.

There were four gates, opening out to the upper city, on the street running parallel to the western wall of the Temple Mount. The most southern of these led up to the Royal Stoa, or basilica, that was erected along the entire southern side of the Mount. It was probably the grandest of the entrances into the entire temple complex, reached by a ramp that passed over the street below. It was also the gate closest to Herod's palace, which adjoined the western wall of the city, and it's likely that he used it as a private entrance to the Royal Stoa. However, the two gates on the southern side leading from the lower city, or City of David, were traditionally the most popular entrances. They too were spectacular; steps led up to a gigantic platform where the gates opened into underground passages that passed under the Royal Stoa and entered directly onto the Court of the Gentiles. The experience of emerging from a dark passage into an expansive plaza lined by classically designed porticos must have been spectacular.

The Royal Stoa, the largest basilica in the Roman Empire, was a centerpiece of the temple project. Josephus wrote that "it was more worthy of mention than any structure under the sun." He was not exaggerating. In fact, expanding the Temple Mount to the south was done expressly to construct the Royal Stoa, and it required the underground arches and vaults to support it. The fact that the entire northern side opened onto the piazza differentiated it from other classical basilicas. The stoa was over a hundred feet wide and almost eight hundred long. There were four rows of columns, forty in each, with the last row embedded into the wall of the Temple Mount. The columns were almost five feet in diameter and thirty feet tall with Corinthian capitals. The four rows of columns provided space for three parallel aisles, the center one twice as high as the others, providing light from windows at the top. The wooden ceilings were adorned with ornate carvings.

Herod had no claim to the high priesthood. Therefore, the Royal Stoa and not the holy sanctuary symbolized his power. He chose to center his rule there and not in his palace. Herod used it to receive official guests, conduct ceremonies, hold receptions, and sit in judgment. While he was not using it, the Royal Stoa was open to the public and it's possible that it was the very location where Jesus overturned the tables of the money changers. The Royal Stoa and the entire Temple Mount became the focal point of Herod's rule, epitomizing his stature as one the great rulers and patrons of the Mediterranean world. The temple itself was designed to attract Jews and gentiles alike. If they did not pass the well-defined boundary lines, limiting their activities to the Court of the Gentiles and the Royal Stoa, gentiles could mingle, gawk, and even sacrifice to the Jewish God. In conclusion, Herod's Temple served a few purposes. It magnified his Jewish authenticity and buttressed his popularity in that community. It helped the economy by employing thousands of workers and bringing visitors from all over the world. Perhaps most significantly, the temple was the most concrete manifestation of Herod's ability to play his role deftly and reach out to his three major constituencies: Romans, Greeks, and Jews.

Chapter 3

The Road to Revolt

HEROD THE GREAT DIED at the age of seventy in March of 4 BCE at his palace in the city of Jericho. His final days were excruciating. Historical forensics suggest that he died of kidney disease and gangrene of the genital area, which induced among other symptoms intense itching, constant breathlessness, and severe convulsions. The time leading up to his death was also psychologically painful, reflecting the dysfunction of his large family that marked most of his reign. Just five days before his demise, Herod executed his eldest son and heir apparent, Antipater, for his involvement in a complex plot to assassinate him. This was especially painful for the dying king. Only a few years before he had also executed his two favorite sons, Alexander and Aristobulus, for conspiring against him. These attractive and popular young men, the sons of his beloved Mariamne, deeply resented him for killing their mother. It never seemed to occur to Herod that uxoricide could inhibit relations with his sons. Besides that, the two princes were inordinately proud of their Hasmonean lineage and despised their other siblings. Their stupidity and pride allowed them to be manipulated by courtiers and other family members, all with their own political agendas.

To complicate matters further, the emperor, Augustus, growing exasperated with his client's inability to control his unruly brood, rescinded his promise that Herod could name his own successor. Herod's final will, contingent on the emperor's approval, named Archelaus, the son of his wife Mathace, a Hellenized Jew from Samaria, as king. Almost immediately after the reading of the will, Archelaus displayed the traits that would ultimately cost him the throne. When riots broke out in Jerusalem, he first leaned toward conciliation and then shifted to ruthless repression, achieving the dubious honor of gaining both disrespect and hatred simultaneously. He journeyed to Rome in order to have his succession approved by Augustus. His brother Antipas, who Herod had named as ruler in the previous will, also rushed there to plead his case. To further complicate the situation, a delegation of Jews, upset by Archelaus's harsh repression of the disorders, proceeded to Rome as well to ask the emperor to impose direct Roman rule. This threat allowed Nicolaus of Damascus, Herod's most trusted advisor and Archelaus's chief advocate, to hammer out a family compromise. Archelaus would rule Judea, Idumea, and Samaria, with his capital in Jerusalem. He received the title of ethnarch from Augustus with the promise he would eventually become king if he performed his duties well. His brother Antipas and half-brother Philip were named as tetrarchs with their own separate domains, the former receiving the rich lands of Galilee and Perea, the region east of the Jordan, and the latter the unruly northeastern regions. Salome, Herod's formidable sister and a close friend of Augustus's wife, Empress Livia, was awarded a few small but rich territories along with a generous financial settlement.

While these machinations were transpiring in Rome, all hell broke loose at home. Riots engulfed Jerusalem. The Roman commander, sent from Syria with troops to maintain the peace, was besieged in Herod's palace, while the insurgents occupied the temple. When the Romans attacked them, the rebels hurled stones and shot arrows from the roofs of the Royal Stoa and the porticos surrounding the Court of the Gentiles. The only way the attackers could dislodge them was by setting fires. The burning cedar beams supporting the roof, melting the gold leafing on the columns, added to the conflagration, taking many lives. Nevertheless, the Jews didn't surrender and kept the Roman general Sabinus hostage in the palace. Risings broke out in the countryside, led by retired veterans, brigands, pretenders, and even distant members of the royal family. One of these was led by the son of the brigand Hezekiah, the very person Herod crucified when his father sent him to rule Galilee. Varus, the governor of Syria, a man who would become infamous a few years later when he lost his own life and three crack legions by ambush in Germany's Teutoberg Forest, acted decisively, marching south from Syria with his two remaining legions. He broke the revolt and made numerous reprisals, including imprisoning many of the rebels and crucifying two thousand of them.

Upon returning home, Archelaus confirmed his ineptitude as a ruler. He was not even able to muster the resources to repair the recent damage to the temple. A delegation of both Jews and Samaritans, usually mortal enemies, formed a united front against him before the emperor in Rome. An exasperated Augustus finally exiled Archelaus to a small city in Gaul on the periphery of the western empire.

Judea would now be ruled directly from Rome. However, direct Roman rule was not the panacea that many Jews hoped it would be. The Romans were often heavy handed, with little sympathy for the distinct Jewish religion and culture. Some Jews even resented that the new prefect, or procurator, came from the equestrian and not the socially more prestigious senatorial class. He reported to the governor of Syria and not directly to the emperor in Rome. The position entailed hard work and intense frustration for minimal prestige. Although the prefect could request military support from the governor of Syria in an emergency, he had to depend on auxiliaries formed from Herod's military establishment, not Roman legionnaires. Often commanded by retired Roman centurions, the ranks were composed mostly of non-Jews from the region. Even though the prefect officially recognized the Sanhedrin as an advisory council and court, his powers were still considerable. He could overrule any legal judgments and his approval was required for executions. The prefect appointed the high priest and administered the temple and its finances. Symbolically important, this Roman official even controlled the priestly vestments, the garments worn on the high holy days. As a diplomatic gesture the prefect ruled from Caesarea, but he came to Jerusalem to keep order during the major religious festivals. This explains Pontius Pilate's presence in Jerusalem for Jesus's trial. Finally, a permanent military force was garrisoned in the Fortress Antonia, which was connected to the temple itself.

The problems of direct rule can be illustrated by the actions of the most well-known Roman prefect, Pontius Pilate. Both the Gospels and Josephus portray him as a mean-spirited, petty tyrant. He governed for ten years, from 26 to 36 CE. Josephus records two incidents that illustrated his heavy-handed incompetence. The first was particularly galling to the Jews. Pilate ordered his troops to march into Jerusalem carrying their standards. This provocative gesture had previously been wisely avoided. The standards comprised medallions showing the image of the emperor, a direct insult to Jewish religious beliefs. The combination of riots in Jerusalem and the refusal of a delegation meeting with him in Caesarea to submit to his violent threats forced Pilate to back down. Most likely he realized that the emperor Tiberius would not look kindly on a prefect who incited revolt in his jurisdiction. In the second case, his initial actions were more reasonable but his response to the ensuing protests in Jerusalem were brutal. He had diverted temple funds, originally earmarked for temple repairs, by then largely complete, to the construction of a sorely needed aqueduct to supply the city with water during droughts. However, Pilate lacked the foresight to perceive that Jews would find the diversion of funds raised for religious purposes to secular ones provocative. Riots broke out in Jerusalem, joined in by a large number of Galileans visiting for a religious festival. The auxiliaries infiltrated the crowds, civilian clothing covering their armor, and cut many of the rioters down. The blood of the victims, it was said, mingled with that of the temple sacrifices.

The Jewish elites, for the most part, cooperated with Rome. Social instability and religious unrest were anathema to them. The long tenure of the high priest Caiaphas that overlapped with most of Pilate's term illustrates this. However, a fundamental contradiction in Roman policy toward the Jews constantly frustrated this shared desire for peace. Most of the time, Rome supported religious liberty for the Jews. They exempted the Jews from emperor worship, which was required as a show of political loyalty throughout the empire. However, the prefect was expected to quell political unrest with maximum force. The Romans never truly understood that religion and politics were one and the same to the Jews. To separate the two was a fool's errand.

Herod Antipas remained as the ruler of Galilee and Perea. Both regions provided substantial revenues, but the Jewish population of Galilee tended to be even more fanatical than their Judean co-religionists. Nevertheless, Antipas ruled firmly in his father's fashion. He attained the respect and trust of the emperor Tiberius, even once being asked to mediate between the Roman governor of Syria and the Parthians. Although he never achieved the love of his people, he did gain their grudging respect. He built two new cities on the Sea of Galilee, one named Tiberius after his patron the emperor, where he also built his major palace. Both cities had Greek constitutions like other hellenized ones in the Roman East, but, unlike the cities his father founded, largely populated by gentiles, these were mainly Jewish. Unlike their counterparts in Judea, the local ruling class welcomed an intermediary to Rome like Antipas, who understood their religion and culture. In the Gospels, these elite Jewish supporters of Antipas were called Herodians and like the Pharisees were perceived as naturally antagonistic to Jesus.

Although Herod Antipas would gain notoriety for his execution of John the Baptist, his ultimate downfall was a result of inheriting a less constructive trait of his father: obsessive love founded on sexual desire. On one of his frequent trips to Rome, he fell madly in love with his half-brother's wife, Herodias. She was also his niece, being the daughter of another half-brother, Aristobulus, the one executed for plotting against his father, Herod. For her part, Herodias was attracted to her much older uncle because her current husband showed absolutely no ambition. She exerted great influence on her new spouse, most of it bad. She encouraged the execution of John the Baptist because the prophet preached against the incestuous and unlawful nature of her marriage. However, even more damaging from a political perspective was her demand that Antipas divorce his first wife, a Nabatean princess. The princess fled to her father in Petra, who would later lead an invasion in revenge. Despite this embarrassment, requiring a plea for Roman aid, Antipas still retained his tetrarchy. He finally lost it in 39 CE when he was exiled to Spain after being accused of treachery against the new emperor, Caligula, ostensibly egged on by his wife.

Philip, known in history as Philip the Tetrarch, by all accounts skillfully ruled his unruly border region northeast of the Sea of Galilee. This region, except for a couple of small pockets, was non-Jewish. It was poorer than both Judea and the realm of Antipas, but in the more settled western region he built two small cities, Julius and Caesarea Paneas, which he inhabited with hellenized gentiles. The more rugged, tribal, eastern region had been pacified by Herod the Great, and Philip maintained the peace and controlled the brigandage by ruling firmly but fairly. He spent almost all his time in the tetrarchy, avoiding visits to the imperial court in Rome. He traveled extensively through his domain, carrying a portable throne with him that could be set up at any time or place to dispense justice. At a late age he married his niece Salome, the daughter of Herodias, infamous for performing the dance that culminated in the execution of John the Baptist. Nevertheless, Philip died childless in 34 CE. His tetrarchy came under direct Roman rule.

Therefore, the land in which Jesus conducted his ministry was not ruled by one single sovereign. It was complex and heterogeneous not only politically, but also socially and culturally. One cannot fully comprehend the Gospels without acknowledging this. Take for example the movements of Jesus recorded in chapters 7 and 8 in the Gospel of Mark. He started in Galilee, which was ruled by Herod Antipas. From there he journeyed northwest to Tyre on the Mediterranean coast. The area was Phoenician but under the jurisdiction of the Roman governor of Syria. He then traveled southwest around or over the Sea of Galilee to the Decapolis, a group of independent city states under Roman protection located in what is now modern-day Jordan. The area was ethnically Semitic, but the cities were hellenized with a strong Roman influence. To add another level of complexity, we need to keep in mind that there were large pockets of Jews in both Phoenicia and the Decapolis. The Jews, not the gentiles, were Jesus's primary audience. From there he briefly returned to Galilee but shortly thereafter sailed across the Sea of Galilee to Bethsaida, which was in Philip's tetrarchy, later incorporated into the province of Syria. And what about Jerusalem, where Jesus would be crucified, and according to John's Gospel, he visited several times during his life? It was in Judea, which, along with Idumea and Samaria, was ruled by a Roman prefect based in Caesarea who in turn reported to the governor of Syria. But Jerusalem was also directly administered by the high priest and his council, the Sanhedrin. Ironically, only a few years before, almost all these territories were under the direct rule or influence of Herod the Great. And not only was the world of Jesus politically diverse, but it was also polyglot. He spoke Aramaic, the lingua franca of the entire Levant, but also Hebrew and perhaps, like many of his countrymen, had a knowledge of Greek.

For all Herod's success, there were two major downsides to his rule. The first is obvious. His inability to control his own family and his deep-seated emotional insecurity ensured that on his death his kingdom would be fractured and weak, not unified and strong. Roman domination and internal stress were inevitable. Second, if the destruction of his enemies and the creation of a new ruling class strengthened the stability of his own regime, it also led to social and economic dislocation after his death. This in turn set the stage for the great Jewish revolt that would lead not only to the complete decimation of Herod's former kingdom, but also the devastation of Jerusalem and the destruction of the beautiful temple he had so recently completed.

The rationale for successful Roman rule of its empire was straightforward. Even though it possessed the best army of the ancient world, Rome did not have the resources or the technology to rule the empire with an iron fist alone. Instead, Rome needed to coopt the provincial ruling class. And the Romans, being a pragmatic but exceedingly ethnocentric people, defined the elite in their own terms. Roman senators, who were at the top of the social hierarchy, were honored for their birth and wealth, both of which provided them with the *dignitas*, or "dignity," to rule. In the provinces, the equivalent to the Roman senatorial class were the urban oligarchies. They possessed the local knowledge necessary to carry out the censuses required to implement taxation. Their local prestige also allowed these elites to help Rome keep the peace and mediate any popular grievances with the governor and in some cases the emperor. For their part, they understood that cooperation with Rome promised concrete benefits. Collecting the taxes often meant a skim off the top. Also present was the incentive of Roman citizenship with all that implied: an opportunity to join the legions and maybe even one day enter the Roman senate, transcending their provincial roots and merging into the imperial ruling class. Most of the time, Rome was correct in assuming that its interests and that of the provincial ruling classes were aligned.

It was not so straightforward in Judea. The Judean ruling class simply did not conform to the prevailing provincial imperial model. Even if a ruling elite existed when Pompey arrived on the scene, it didn't reflect the attributes that Rome expected. Status depended neither on wealth nor ownership of land, but rather on religious prestige. To make matters worse, Herod the Great, the ruthless Hellenistic monarch that he was, made it his goal to tie the elites to him, the sole dispenser of wealth and privilege. This required the eradication of the Hasmonean ruling class. He surrounded himself with those he could trust, mostly gentiles, Idumeans, and members of his own family, people universally despised by the general population. Moreover, since he did not have the lineage to be high priest himself, Herod had to make certain that the holders of the office were nonentities and not a political threat to him. When Rome took direct control of Judea in 6 CE, it correctly perceived the high priesthood as the apex of the provincial ruling class, but there was no one available with the prestige and lineage required to gain universal respect. Instead, Ananias, the patriarch of a wealthy but obscure family, was chosen. His relatives (including Caiaphas, his son in law who presided over the trial of Jesus) and descendants would virtually control the office until the onset of the great revolt. They attempted to cooperate with the imperial authorities, but the people looked at them with contempt, perceiving them to be creatures of Rome. Most likely the negative connotation of Caiaphas and the Sanhedrin, implicit in the Gospels during the trial of Jesus, reflects this popular antipathy against the elite rather than being anti-Jewish.

It was this structural fracture in the social fabric, the lack of a viable and respected ruling class, that the eminent Oxford historian Martin Goodman argues was the chief cause of the Jewish revolt. It was not simply Roman oppression or an inevitable clash between religious and national identities. Josephus, for his part, blamed the revolt on the lawlessness and impudence of the lower classes, but he was not an objective observer. His family was a part of the temple elite. Bottom line: The members of the ruling class lacked the prestige required to help the Romans rule. Consequently, their imperial bosses disdained them for this, making it impossible for the Jewish elite to break into the Roman imperial hierarchy. And ironically, the Jews themselves, because of their own religious exceptionalism, had no desire to assimilate with their conquerors. Not a formula for success.

Such a situation was not sustainable. A blowup was inevitable. The only possible way to contain it was a reinstatement of Herodian rule over the entire region. At least the offspring of Herod the Great were Jews and, if not loved by their people, knew what it took to maintain control. One such contender was Herod's grandson Herod Agrippa, the son of the executed Aristobulus. His lineage could not have been better, especially since his grandmother Mariamne was a Hasmonean princess. Moreover, if Herod the Great cut his teeth crucifying bandits in Galilee, his grandson earned his credentials in a place in its own way even more treacherous, the imperial court in Rome. He was bold, charming, and unscrupulous, charismatic but manipulative. If he lacked his grandfather's wanton cruelty, he made up for it with his shameless, impetuous, and brazen ambition. Agrippa certainly was more pleasant company, suave and charming, than his grandfather but Herod, with all his rough edges, had the makings of the better king.

Herod Agrippa's ups and downs, his narrow escapes and rise to a grandeur no one would have expected, culminating with a dramatic and tragic death, are the stuff of a television mini-series. His father was executed in 7 BCE when his son was only three years old. His mother, Berenice, the daughter of Herod's formidable sister Salome, whisked the young prince to Rome, where they received the protection of both the Empress Livia and her daughter-in-law Antonia, the daughter of Mark Anthony and Augustus's sister Octavia. Antonia was also the mother of the future emperor

Claudius and, next to Livia, the most powerful woman in Rome. As he grew up, Agrippa used all his charm to insinuate his way into the imperial family and the upper reaches of Roman society. He never understood the value of money; to him it was just a means to win friends and influence people. Nevertheless, while his mother lived, he was forced to control his spending, but on her death, he lost all restraint, squandered his patrimony, and went into debt. Agrippa tested even the patience of the emperor Tiberius, who generally liked him but hated his prodigality. He had to slip out of Rome leaving behind many angry creditors.

Things moved quickly after his return to his homeland. Depressed, he attempted suicide, but his wife—not surprisingly for his family, a first cousin—convinced her husband's sister Herodias to bring him into the court of her husband Herod Antipas. Agrippa chaffed under the grudging generosity of his uncle. In a fit of drunken rage, he told him off, burning his bridges there completely. Agrippa fled to Syria and ingratiated himself there with the Roman governor. Syria, however, was the turf of Agrippa's younger brother who jealously accused him of taking bribes. Matters only got worse. Agrippa fled to Alexandria intent on booking a passage back to Rome. However, detained there for his debts in Rome, he bribed his guards and sailed to Italy. Back in Rome, his mother's old friend Antonia bailed him out by paying off his creditors. Then Agrippa aimed his attention at his boyhood friend, the nephew of Antonia and likely heir to Tiberius, Caligula. But he almost blew it all. Hosting Caligula for dinner, Agrippa raised his arms to the heavens, praying that the emperor would die soon so his friend Caligula, so much more qualified, could rule in his stead. When word of this reached Tiberius, he was infuriated. Only the intervention of Agrippa's patron and the emperor's sister-in-law, Antonia, saved him from execution. But it was touch and go until fate intervened. Tiberius died and Caligula became emperor. Suddenly, Herod Agrippa's luck changed.

First, the new emperor awarded his close friend the tetrarchy of Philip, which had reverted to direct Roman rule on his death. On his way there, Agrippa stopped in Alexandria where the large Jewish population was beleaguered by the Greek majority, who had drawn the Roman governor Flaccus to their side. Agrippa sent a message to Caligula, subtly implying that the emperor's dignity was being challenged. This was partly responsible for Flaccus's arrest and recall. This greatly increased his credibility with the Jews in the east. Another incident reinforced his popularity with the Jews. Egged on by the gentiles of Jamnia, a city near the coast just south of present-day Tel Aviv, and the current Roman prefect, Caligula ordered that a larger-than-life-sized statue of him dressed as Zeus be placed in the temple's Holy of Holies. This was a sure recipe for disaster, a certain catalyst for revolt. The real hero of the affair was the Roman governor of Syria, Petronius, who wisely procrastinated and urged the emperor to reconsider, but Agrippa, in Rome at the time, added his own advice and later took most of the credit for himself, even though it was the assassination of Caligula that really brought the affair to its end. Before that, however, Agrippa, ever the master manipulator, used his sister Herodias's excessive ambition against her and her husband Antipas. He accused them of treachery against the emperor, engineering their exile and the award of their dominions to himself.

His most adroit maneuvering, however, came immediately after the assassination of Caligula in 41 CE. Still in Rome, he astutely sided with Claudius, the son of his old patron Antonia, who had been declared emperor by the praetorian guard. Claudius had a stutter and was socially maladroit, causing most people to believe him mentally impaired, but there were no other adult males of the Julio-Claudian line available. Some senators wanted a return to the republic, but the day had long passed when such an option would be viable. Josephus and the Roman historian Tacitus give different accounts, the former most likely exaggerating Agrippa's role in supporting Claudius, but the new emperor must have appreciated his Jewish friend's help. He added to Agrippa's realm and gave him the title of king. He now ruled an area roughly the size of his grandfather's, including the areas that had been under direct Roman rule, making it the richest and most prestigious client kingdom of Rome's eastern empire. Despite the opinions of many in Rome, Claudius was no fool. He realized that direct rule had not been successful, with the risks greater than the rewards. Perhaps a client king would bring the peace and stability that a Roman prefect could not.

Herod Agrippa's reign was glorious, extravagant, and short. In some respects, it mirrored that of his grandfather Herod the Great's. He sought the support of his Jewish population, building on the good will achieved by his defense of the Alexandrian Jews and his maneuvers to stop Caligula's statue from polluting the Holy of Holies. Like his grandfather, Agrippa stipulated that male gentiles marrying a member of his family needed to be circumcised. He also cultivated the Pharisees and cracked down on the new Christian cult. On the other hand, he adopted the persona of a Hellenistic monarch, appealing to his gentile and more cosmopolitan Jewish subjects. Not only did he put his own image on his coins, something Herod the Great even avoided, but he also built baths, pagan temples, theaters, and amphitheaters that staged musical competitions and even gladiatorial games. Furthermore, Agrippa lacked self-discipline and allowed his vanity to control his actions. For all his faults, Herod the Great understood one very important truth: Keep Rome happy. His grandson, however, took his relationship with Rome for granted. Two examples illustrate this. He began to build new walls around Jerusalem to protect the new city, north of the temple. The governor of Syria informed the emperor Claudius, who ordered his wayward protégé to desist immediately. He also convened a conference in the Galilean city of Tiberius with all the major client kings on the boundaries of the eastern empire. His motivation was probably not sinister, rather a manifestation of his own sense of importance, but the rebuke from the governor of Syria was swift and to the point. The kings were ordered home. Finally, the description of Herod Agrippa's sudden demise in 44 CE by Josephus is the stuff of Greek tragedy. On the second day of the magnificent athletic games honoring the deceased Emperor Augustus hosted by him, Agrippa became mortally ill, dying a few days later of a sickness much like the one that killed his grandfather. Josephus blames hubris. When his magnificent jewel-studded attire caused the people to praise him as a god, Agrippa did not demur.

His son Herod Agrippa II was also brought up in the imperial court. He would be placated with a patchwork of small dominions outside of Judea by Claudius without the title of king. However, he was awarded control of the temple in Jerusalem with the right to appoint the high priest, and this significantly raised his prestige among Jews. His sister Berenice, later the consort of the future emperor Titus, was his chief confidant and rumored incestuous lover. His other sister Drusilla married the Roman procurator Felix. Agrippa and Berenice remained true to their people. They tried to nip the incipient revolt with all its disastrous consequences in the bud but would ultimately stay loyal to Rome.

Herod Agrippa's life and legend had a profound impact on the generation that would lead the Jewish revolt. The affair of the standards along with other Roman miscues and his brief but superficially glorious reign took on mythical proportion, emphasizing not only Roman oppression but also lionizing the rule of a Jewish king. If the Jews had their own sovereigns in the recent past, why wouldn't it be possible to achieve it for the future? What seems inevitable now, the Roman suppression of the great revolt, did not appear so at the time. Taking our knowledge of historical outcomes to argue inevitability is always dangerous.

Brigandage in the countryside and urban terrorism in Jerusalem increased in the 50s CE. The procurators (this term had replaced prefect) were unable to and perhaps uninterested in stemming the rising violence. Indeed, the procurator governing at the beginning of that decade was sent back to Rome when he failed to quell riots that were exacerbated by a "Robin Hood" like folk hero operating in the region between Judea and Samaria. However, whereas brigandage, or banditry, had always been endemic to the countryside, its urban counterpart, fostered by gangs of sicarii, or knife men, was a newer phenomenon. These ruffians were particularly frightening. They would approach the intended victim in a crowded area with their daggers hidden under a cloak, disappearing back into the crowd before anyone realized anything had happened. Popular historians have confused them with the Zealots, one of the factions leading the rebellion, but they were more nebulous and amorphous. Like the brigands in the countryside there was a religious element involved. They probably were followers of what Josephus called the Fourth Philosophy, the belief that there should be no ruler but God. However, in the period leading up to the revolt they were mainly employed by the political factions vying for power and influence in Jerusalem. There's even evidence suggesting that the former high priest and richest and most powerful man in Jerusalem, Ananias, supported and used them. Not only did they do the bidding of the ruling elite but they also at times acted in the interests of the Roman authorities. Brigands in the countryside displayed similar attributes. Later, during the revolt in Galilee, they supported leaders who were in fact fighting a civil war between themselves much like the faction leaders in Jerusalem. We tend to classify historical figures and groups in modern terms, leading to anachronistic oversimplifications that suggest clear cut motives and aims that simply didn't exist. However, if I were trying to explain the sicarii to a modern audience I would try this: Imagine members of the Taliban hiring themselves out to the highest bidder on the mean streets of Kabul.

The procurator Albinus (62 to 64 CE) was particularly venal and incompetent. He gladly accepted bribes from the incredibly wealthy ex-High Priest Ananias, and other members of high priestly families, and from the elite secular families involved in the conflict between political factions. The stakes are unclear to us now, but the intensity of the factional conflict indicate that they were very real. Nevertheless, it should be emphasized that there is no evidence suggesting that any of this conflict involved religious ideology; it was over raw political power, pure and simple. In any event, it paid to incentivize the procurator to turn a blind eye to breaches of the peace. Indeed, when a group of sicarii kidnapped the secretary of Ananias's son Eleazar, the powerful captain of the temple, they were correct in assuming that this would provide them with significant leverage. They pretended to blackmail Ananias. He in turn bribed the procurator, who released a few sicarii from prison. It was all a setup. Ananias talked peace but secretly supported the sicarii against Rome. Revolt was simmering beneath the surface in all layers of society.

It was Florus, the next procurator, however, who ignited this smoldering cauldron and incited revolt. Tensions in Caesarea boiled over in 66 CE when rioting broke out between Jews and gentiles. Florus accepted bribes from the Jews but supported the Greeks instead. He exacerbated the situation by seizing the large sum of seventeen talents from the temple treasury. The procurator had some justification for this—the province was behind on its tribute—but it was a politically inept move. The Jews saw it as sacrilege, but ironically it was a joke that turned a volatile situation into open revolt. During demonstrations against the pillage of the treasury, several youths started passing around baskets asking for copper coins to help the "poor starveling," a sarcastic reference to Florus. He demanded that the youths be handed over. The Jewish leaders apologized but refused to meet his demand. Incensed, the procurator let his troops loose on the population and kidnapped some wealthy citizens of Jerusalem, executing several of them. More and more it appeared that Rome, represented by this venal and incompetent official, was no longer protecting Jewish interests. The unrest intensified, forcing Florus to flee to Caesarea. Agrippa II and his sister Berenice attempted to calm the crowds but to no avail. Eleazar, the son of Ananias, used his power as captain of the temple to halt sacrifices on behalf of the emperor. This highly symbolic and provocative act announced an irrevocable breach with Rome. It was a master stroke of propaganda. It symbolized the purification of the temple, a rallying cry for a large segment of the Jewish population. His father publicly opposed the action but secretly encouraged it. It is not uncommon in periods of revolt or civil war for families to hedge their bets by supporting both sides. Unfortunately, in this case the consequences would be tragic for the family.

Within four years Jerusalem would be sacked and the temple destroyed. The world as Jesus knew would be obliterated; the world in which the Gospels were written, and Christianity grew, would emerge. Events moved quickly toward this tragic conclusion, but if to us the ending appears inevitable, to many of the Jewish people the opposite was true, and the initial events confirmed their optimism. It is not our intent to describe the actual revolt in detail, but its initial eruption is instructive. It provides a snapshot of the political and social environment, providing insight into the world of Jesus.

The ruling elite was still split on the question of revolt. Some of the chief priests, in a meeting of the people held in the outer temple court, pointed out that even their ancestors didn't object to gentiles presenting offerings, arguing that sacrifices to the emperor were not inherently sacrilegious. Ananias on his part pretended to support them. Most of his faction had no idea he was one of the masterminds of the revolt. Ananias didn't want to show his cards until the revolt reached the point of no return. New archeological evidence strongly implies that he was involved in the seizure of Masada and the large supply of weapons and armor stored there. In any event, riots broke out that soon turned into open civil war. The pro-revolt faction controlled the temple and the Lower City, which included the Ophel, or City of David. Their opponents, favoring peace with Rome, occupied the Upper City west of the temple where both the old Hasmonean palace and Herod's palace were situated. Heavy fighting continued for a week but there was a lull for the Feast of Wood Carrying, when the populace brought wood to the temple for the sacrifices at the altar. When the unarmed crowds entered the temple, a riot broke out between the factions. A group of sicarii, supporting the insurgent and probably summoned by Eleazar, mingled in with the crowd and began killing their opponents. This was the tipping point. The fighting spilled out of the temple and into the Upper City, driving out both the peace faction and Agrippa's troops. The insurgents, oblivious of his secret support, burned down Ananias's house and partially incinerated the Hasmonean palace, Agrippa's home in the city. They also destroyed the public record office, burning all credit records, aiming to gain the support of a multitude of debtors in the country. The Antonia Fortress was overcome in two days and its garrison massacred. The peace faction made a final stand in Herod's palace, the citadel of the city.

At this point events take an intriguing turn that illustrates the social tensions underlying the revolt. Suddenly a messianic brigand leader named Menahem enters the stage. His lineage is almost too good to be true, and for that reason alone Josephus probably didn't make it up. His grandfather was

Judas the Galilean who had led a revolt against the census implemented by Rome in 6 CE when it took direct control of Judea. According to Josephus, Judas espoused a messianic creed called the Fourth Philosophy, which professed that the Jews should have no ruler except for God. His father, or perhaps grandfather, was the brigand Hezekiah who Herod the Great had executed in Galilee. All three men represented not only the continuing problem of banditry in Galilee but also its close connection to religion. They saw no contradiction between slitting a man's throat, either Jew or gentile, and religious purity.

Menahem acted decisively. He took a band of his sicarii followers to Masada and persuaded the garrison installed there by Ananias to hand over the armaments stored to support the rebels besieging Herod's palace in Jerusalem. The possession of these weapons allowed Menahem to take over command of the siege. The fighting was intense. The defenders, however, saw the futility of resistance and negotiated a truce that allowed Agrippa's troops and most of the besieged to leave. Menahem, however, became even more ruthless and aggressive. Any defenders who hadn't left the palace quickly enough were butchered in cold blood. The Roman auxiliary troops fell back to the three great towers built by Herod but were overwhelmed. Finally, and must dramatically, his brigand followers tracked down Ananias and butchered him. This duplicitous power broker had overplayed his hand. He was waiting for just the right tactical moment to declare his leadership of the revolt but waited too long. Revolutions often devour their own.

Ananias's son Eleazar might have condoned the burning of his father's house, but not his murder. It was time for the elite to turn on the interloper. Shortly thereafter, when Menahem entered the temple with his supporters to worship, announcing his messianic pretensions by dressing as a king, the populous led by Eleazar attacked them. Overwhelmed, Menahem and his armed men ran for it. Most were cut down, while a few fled to Masada. He was captured in the Ophel district of the Old City and tortured to death.

The die was cast. The revolt would continue, but it would be run by the ruling class. The leaders of the peace faction had been virtually eliminated by Menahem. These events underlined the dynamics of the revolt. Even though there would be continued factional conflict, the elites retained control. Bandits, sicarii, and tough Idumean troops would all play a part, but they were the puppets controlled by their masters. And during the factional conflict that continued almost to the very end, it was political power not religious ideology that was at stake. Indeed, the barbaric execution of

Menahem indicates that messianic fanaticism was not welcome by the revolutionary elite. You will not find the story of Ananias's duplicity in Josephus. It has been pieced together by using archeological evidence and a careful reading of the text by a modern historian, Michael Owen Wise. Ananias's role did not fit Josephus's argument that the revolution came from below, not above. The historian was a member of the high priestly class and did not want to admit its culpability in bringing on disaster.

Responsibility for quelling the outbreak of revolt lay with the governor of Syria, Cestius Gallus. During the summer of 66 CE, he prepared to move south to Jerusalem. The core of his force was the Twelfth Legion, about six thousand men, but it also included components of two other legions under his control. This force was supported by auxiliaries raised from client kings, including Agrippa. Meanwhile, bloody clashes between Jews and gentiles were breaking out across Palestine.

Cestius Gallus marched into Galilee and ravaged the countryside to strike fear into the rebels. The massacres continued as he moved down the coast en route to Jerusalem. His forces reached the city in October and assaulted the northern wall. Gallus realized at that point he did not possess the forces necessary to take the city. He decided to retreat to the coast and return the next year with reinforcements. The one thing he didn't expect was an enemy attack, believing that no ragtag rebel army could match the disciplined Roman legionaries in the open field. Overconfidence resulted in disaster. As his forces marched in a disorderly fashion through the Bethoron Pass, the Jews attacked and annihilated the Romans. Six thousand troops were killed and, even more disturbing, the rebels captured the eagle standard of the Twelfth Legion, a profoundly humiliating outcome for any Roman commander. Up to this point the unrest in Judea had represented a local threat necessitating police action. Gallus had never believed that he would be refused entry to Jerusalem in the first place. The destruction of a Roman army lifted instability to another level: a revolt of an entire province. This was a direct assault on the emperor in Rome, the prestige of the empire itself.

Realizing the seriousness of the situation, the emperor Nero named a tough old general by the name Vespasian as the Roman commander. He was the perfect choice. Vespasian had showed his military acumen twenty years earlier in the conquest of Britain. As a legate, he commanded the legion that pacified the southwest of the island. Although he held senatorial rank and his family, the Flavians, were well connected, Vespasian was a "new man"; his father, the son of a centurion, had been an equestrian and not a member of the old aristocracy. In other words, he was a safe bet, wrongly perceived as a threat neither to the emperor nor any future contenders for imperial power.

Vespasian arrived on the scene at the beginning of the next year. He commanded three legions, auxiliary troops, and detachments from client kingdoms. He assembled a strong staff, including his twenty-seven-year-old son Titus, who commanded one of the legions. He moved first into Galilee where he reduced the opposition by taking one hilltop stronghold after another. His goal was not so much to secure his flank but rather to strike fear and awe into the defenders of Jerusalem, his ultimate target. Josephus, who had been appointed commander of the rebels in Galilee, surrendered when Jotapata fell, choosing that over joining a mass suicide. He later said that his prophecy that Vespasian would become emperor saved his life. John of Gishala, a Galilean, took over the command in the region and put up a stiff resistance. However, he was forced to retreat to Jerusalem, where he would be one of the key faction leaders in the beleaguered city.

Two exogenous events slowed the Roman advance and gave the Jews in Judea a breathing spell. The first was the death of Nero in June of 68 CE. This forced Vespasian to cease operations because his imperial mandate had lapsed. When he finally prepared to move on Jerusalem in the spring of 69 CE, his troops proclaimed him emperor. This necessitated a postponement of hostilities while he moved on Rome to seize the prize.

This respite would allow the Jews to set up a functioning state. The courts met, sacrifices at the temple continued, and a fine silver currency was minted. It also provided an environment for ruthless political infighting between the various factions. John of Gishala sided with the Zealots on his return. The Zealots have been confused with the sicarii by many popular historians and writers who anachronistically applied this appellation to any fanatics opposing Roman occupation. The Zealots came into existence in 68 CE when they took over after the defeats in Galilee. They were not fanatics from the lower strata of society, but rather well born priests "zealous" for the temple cult. Some of the faction that the Zealots ousted from power fled to the country and joined Simon of Gioras, another leader from the ruling class, who had gained success with his guerrilla tactics against Cestius Gallus. He had left Jerusalem because of his opposition to Ananias. Simon returned to Jerusalem with his supporters and a large contingent of Idumean troops, seizing most of the city. The Zealots continued to hold the

Inner Temple and John of Gishala its outer precincts. The three factions remained at loggerheads for a year until the Romans surrounded Jerusalem in the spring of 70 CE.

We don't have detailed knowledge of how each of these groups recruited their followers. The attraction of the Zealots, representing the temple elite, is relatively clear, but what drew people to John and Simon is less obvious. People who flocked to Jerusalem from Galilee had a natural inclination to join John of Gishala, one of their own. Simon attracted followers from Samaria and the Idumeans seemed to have perceived him as a more effective leader. In fact, people did not follow any leader for religious or ideological reasons. They represented cults of personality. Everyone, leaders and followers alike, had similar views in respect to their religion and their opposition to the Romans.

When Vespasian headed to Rome to seize imperial power, Titus took command of his father's legions. As he approached Jerusalem, his forces consisted of four legions plus auxiliaries. The size of the Roman army underlines the respect they held for their adversaries. The Jews were fierce warriors and Jerusalem was nearly impregnable. Neither a port or a commercial crossroads, Jerusalem was built in hill country, its priority defense. It was well stocked with grain and livestock. Large cisterns were filled with water. Attacking armies, on the other hand, were forced to forage in a countryside devoid of rich agricultural land. Water was not easy to procure, especially during the scorching summer. Jerusalem was positioned at the summit of the Judean hills that ran north to south through Palestine. A few of the elevations within the city were well over two thousand feet above sea level, and a deep valley protected the eastern walls, including the Temple Mount, while a shallower one ringed the western walls. An attack from the south or east was virtually impossible and from the other two directions extremely difficult. The original walls enclosed the Lower and Upper Cities, the ancient heart of Jerusalem. The northwest corner was buttressed by the citadel that consisted of Herod's palace and the three great towers he built. The northeast corner was strengthened by the Temple Mount itself with the Antonia Fortress next to it. The Hasmoneans had added a second wall protecting the areas north of the first one, intersecting with the citadel and the Antonia. Beyond that, enclosing the new city was a third wall, the one begun by Agrippa I. He had been ordered not to complete it, but the rebels finished it before the Romans arrived. The city was certainly a hard nut to crack, and any assault would cost thousands of lives on both sides. Titus had the option of just sitting there, waiting to end the siege by starvation. Much of the grain supply in the city had been destroyed by fire during internecine fighting between the Jewish factions. However, a long siege was not in the cards. Vespasian ordered Titus to make a direct assault, no matter the cost in Roman lives. After the death of Nero, three contenders in the space of a year had vied for the imperial throne. After seizing power each in turn was overthrown and killed. All of them came from older and more prestigious senatorial families than the new emperor. What he needed badly was the propaganda value of a great and glorious victory culminated by a magnificent triumph displaying priceless spoils of war and thousands of prisoners. The Flavians could not be perceived as starving out a ragtag mob of provincial rebels. For maximum impact they needed a narrative that portrayed a great victory over a proud and fierce nation, which was, ironically, not far from the truth.

Titus built his main camp facing the west wall, north of the citadel, overlooking the Hinnom Valley. He ordered a smaller camp to be constructed across from the more imposing Kidron Valley and directly opposite the Temple Mount. The fighting was fierce. The defenders sortied out of the city several times, twice almost killing Titus, who was forced to fight for his life. The Romans would build siege towers and earthworks to breech the fortifications. The Jews would destroy them, forcing the attackers to construct new ones. In May, Titus breached the western segment of the weaker outer third wall enclosing the new city. At this point Titus ordered his own wall built around the entire city. This cut off any supplies coming in and halted the outward flow of refugees. Anyone caught fleeing the city was crucified in plain sight of the defenders or was mutilated and sent back.

His next target would be the keys to the defense of Jerusalem, the Antonia Fortress and the temple itself. But first the Romans needed to breach the stronger second Hasmonean wall. This was accomplished and by June the Antonia fell and was leveled to the ground. This left the temple vulnerable. In August, after bitter fighting, the Jews there were either slaughtered or driven out of the sacred precincts. Titus directed the temple to be sacked and burned. Herod's palace, the citadel, remained in rebel hands, but in view of the helplessness of the situation, fighting petered out. Jerusalem was destroyed. Only Herod's three great towers would be left standing as a monument to commemorate the strength of the city and greatness of the victory. Vespasian and Titus got their extravagant triumph. Finally, the complicity of the members of the Jewish ruling class in the revolt gave Rome no reason to trust them. They were destroyed.

From our perspective the Jewish revolt has a sense of tragic inevitability. How could the leaders of the Jews have even entertained the notion that a successful outcome was at all possible? Therefore, Josephus's argument that the ruling class lost control of events and the revolt was in effect commandeered by fanatics, including the sicarii, from the lower orders still resonates today. However, the participation of perhaps the most influential member of the ruling class, Ananias the former high priest, and his family belies this interpretation. This view does not represent the consensus, but I believe the evidence supports it. Remember that Herod the Great ruled a strong and prosperous client kingdom and Herod Agrippa came close to replicating it. Moreover, as we shall see in the next chapters, the Jews had a strong cultural and political identity matched only by Rome itself. This was not only reinforced by a constitution based on temple and Torah, but also reflected the intense messianic and apocalyptic elements lurking beneath the surface. In our eyes freedom from Rome might seem to be an impossible dream. However, in the eyes of first century Jews, it seemed achievable. Indeed, Josephus, for all his later regrets and rationalizations, initially participated in the revolt and was one of its leaders.

Chapter 4

Society

WE HAVE ALREADY LEARNED some things about the society in which Jesus lived. First, it was a world full of bandits, especially in Galilee. Brigandage, as it was commonly termed, was an amorphous combination of violence and theft with political and religious undertones. The parable of the good Samaritan becomes even more vivid when we understand that this phenomenon was endemic and the road from Jerusalem to Jericho was a particularly notorious spot for just such events. The Roman authorities just didn't care most of the time. The urban centers were the key to imperial administration and the main sources for tribute and taxation. Brigandage also served as a social safety valve. Dispossessed peasants had few other options. The brigand bands were still part of the rural social network, having almost a Robin Hood quality. Only if the Romans were directly impacted did they act, when for example, as Josephus relates, an imperial slave was attacked and robbed by brigands, or if rural unrest had the potential to turn into open revolt. Jesus needed his disciples as bodyguards as well as disciples.

It has also become apparent that Jesus's world was incredibly complex. While he preached, he moved from one political jurisdiction to another. From the tetrarchy of Herod Antipas to that of Philip on the other side of the Sea of Galilee. From Syria and the Decapolis to Judea under a Roman prefect. Numerous languages and dialects were spoken, mainly Aramaic, Greek, and Hebrew. There were large pockets of gentiles, both hellenized and of Semitic origin, throughout ancient Palestine. Then there were the Samaritans. Although they shared religious beliefs with the Jews, there was a profound hatred between the two peoples. The position of Samaria between Judea and Galilee further exacerbated this volatile situation. Josephus viewed the three most important pockets of Jewish population, the nuclei of the Jewish people, to be situated in three areas: Judea, Galilee, and Perea, the semi-arid Transjordan region. The fact is that Jesus navigated a multidimensional world in an almost seamless fashion. Nevertheless, when we consider the proximity of Jew and gentile, even within the major areas of Jewish settlement, it is not difficult to empathize with the Pharisees who built a closed system based on the law to protect themselves from religious impurity. If physical barriers did not exist, social ones were critical, if not indispensable.

As noted earlier, the social fabric of the rural countryside had been torn apart. The soil of Judea, Samaria, and Galilee was not particularly fertile. It could support the cultivation of vines and olives but couldn't produce enough grain to feed the peasant population and supply the needs of Jerusalem. The coastal plain was more fertile, but that area was not predominantly Jewish. Moreover, Judean and Galilean peasants received no benefit from the lush orchards of the Jordan Valley, mostly owned by the Herodians, or the rich balsam groves there, an imperial monopoly. In stark contrast to the countryside, the city of Jerusalem was incredibly rich. A renowned Roman author of that time, Pliny the Elder, said of Jerusalem that it was "the most illustrious city of the East, not just Judea." It was a city that produced luxury goods, such as fine glass, and contained royal palaces and mansions for the rich ruling class. But it was the temple that attracted visitors from all over the ancient world. One of the great religious and tourist sites of the time, it drew incredible wealth into the city.

This great divide between the poor in the countryside and the urban rich was a catalyst for unrest and instability. One example: The elites in Jerusalem, the new ruling class, required investment opportunities for their excess wealth. It was difficult to buy land for investment since there was limited supply, but it could be acquired by forfeiture for outstanding debt. Money was loaned to peasant farmers with their land as collateral. Usury was prohibited in the Torah, but legal technicalities had been developed to get around the prohibition against charging interest. A more serious obstacle was the stipulation in the Torah that loans would be forgiven every seven years. Its intent was to help the poor, but in practice it meant no one would want to make loans, especially close to the seventh or Sabbatical Year. A novel legal instrument, called a *prosbul*, was invented around the time of Jesus to bypass this stipulation. The debtor agreed to waive all rights to forgiveness of debts. It was apparent, however, that the creditor was not interested at all in being paid interest. He desired a default, thus allowing him to acquire the land. The new landlord could choose to keep the farmer on as a tenant, but it was usually more cost effective to work the land with slaves or hire day laborers. One can only imagine the impact on rural society of this convention and the unpopularity that it engendered. The peasant was placed in an impossible economic situation. Facing bankruptcy after a poor harvest, his only recourse was to take out a loan that both he and the creditor knew would almost certainly never be replayed. No wonder that during the insurgency the rebels in Jerusalem, many of whom were displaced farmers, burned down the public record office where these transactions were recorded.

Knowledge of the crisis in the countryside sheds light on one of Jesus's most perplexing parables. The parable of the dishonest steward recounted in Luke has confused readers over the centuries. It tells of a steward who steals from his master, most likely an absentee landlord, and gets caught. The man is petrified. He abhors physical labor and fears the shame of begging. He finds an elegant solution. He'll lower, or in modern parlance, restructure the debts of his master's tenants so they would be bound by honor to support him after he's fired. To the steward's, and the reader's, great surprise, the master, and by implication Jesus, commends him for being shrewd even though it appears to be economically disadvantageous to the owner. Biblical scholars have debated the meaning of the parable, searching for clues to explain the central paradox. Why would Jesus praise a dishonest man? If we view the parable through the eyes of a first century Jew, the meaning is more evident. It concerns the evils of rural debt. The master, the absentee landlord, was wise and righteous enough to allow the lowering of the debt, saving his tenants from destruction, even if the motives of his servant were impure. The parable uses social criticism to support spiritual insight.

However, it was not the emergence of the *prosbul* alone that contributed to the fraying of the social matrix. Overpopulation was also a key factor. Jews took seriously the injunction in Genesis to "be fruitful and multiply." Unlike other ancient societies, abortion and infanticide were prohibited. Moreover, in Roman and Greek culture charity was not a moral or ethical mandate, but rather part of the client/patron relationship. Beggars did not flood the streets of Rome because people didn't feel compelled to give to them. They either died or left the city. Judaism, however, compelled Jews to provide charity to the poor. Not in the modern sense of getting them back on their feet so they can be economically productive members of society, but simply to keep them alive. Multiply the figure in the parable of Lazarus begging outside the rich man's house by thousands and you will get a sense of what the streets of Jerusalem were like.

Legal customs relating to inheritance and land tenure exacerbated the problem. The eldest son received a double share of land and the rest was divided between his brothers, ensuring that holdings became smaller and smaller, making them economically unsustainable, thus increasing the pool of landless workers. Dispossessed peasants did not have many viable options. They could join the Jewish diaspora, but this required financial capital or family abroad willing to support the move. Landless men might also join the bands of brigands roaming the countryside. This certainly didn't result in the social stigma that modern readers would expect, but it did add to the unrest leading up to the revolt. Finally, they could join the urban proletariat in Jerusalem, and some might even become recruits for the sicarii.

Family cohesion was also diminishing. Tribal identity was lost during the Babylonian exile, replaced by family networks. The Torah rested authority in the extended family in the hands of autocratic patriarchs. However, by the time of Jesus, the power of these patriarchs had diminished, and nuclear families had become the norm. The disappearance of tribal identity made this inevitable. The shrinkage of land holdings further disrupted these extended networks and encouraged their replacement by nuclear units. Consequently, endogamy, or marriage within an extended family or tribal unit, had virtually disappeared. Therefore, people looked for economic and social help from close family or neighbors, not from a distant relative.

Even within the nuclear family, the male head saw his authority weaken. No longer was his power unchallenged. Remember that Eleazar, the son of Ananias, defied his father when he ordered sacrifices to the emperor halted. And as we will see in the next chapter, the Essenes encouraged their members to rebel against parental authority. Even the teachings, and indeed the actions, of Jesus encouraged his followers to leave their families. The impact of this trend had ramifications beyond family dynamics. The judges in the villages were the respected patriarchal figures. Their stature and good sense were the basis of their authority. They were expected to keep the peace. The absentee landlords lived in their city mansions, rarely visiting their holdings. The Romans really didn't care what happened in these small towns and villages if their power and the flow of revenues were not affected. If the prestige of these elders was diminishing within their own families, it had to weaken their local authority. This left an opening for learned men like the Pharisees to step into the void. They were the ones who challenged Jesus, not the village elders. However, their focus was on religious law, not keeping the communal peace.

This general weakening of the family and patriarchal authority did have at least one positive impact. Still oppressed by modern standards, women appear to have gained more independence. If we refer to the rabbinic teachings of a century or two after our period, both marriage and divorce appear relatively straightforward and favored the interests of the husband above those of the wife. The woman had no choice in the matter. Her father would choose who she would marry. Once a betrothal took place, the couple were legally joined. Consummation usually occurred later. A betrothal could take place in three different ways: a monetary payment, a contract, or simple cohabitation. Neither partner had the option of breaking it, even with a monetary payment. Divorce was legal, expressly allowed in the Torah, but solely at the discretion of the husband, who could initiate it for almost any reason. Joseph, according to Matthew, considered doing just that, albeit in a kindly fashion, when he learned of Mary's pregnancy. If there were children, they stayed with the father, and he had no legal responsibility to support his former wife. Finally, there were some specific guidelines. Priests needed to marry women from priestly families to keep their lineage pure, and the Pharisees were adamant that no Jew should marry a gentile. Polygamy was not prohibited, but it was certainly frowned upon, as was concubinage. And although sexual exploitation of female slaves likely existed, it was considered socially reprehensible, reflecting a more humane notion of slavery than other ancient peoples.

However, the description of marriage in the rabbinic texts represented an ideal, not the reality. They reflect a notion of a strong patriarchal society that, as we have seen, no longer existed. As is often the case in history, the reality was much more complex. On the surface it appeared that the husband totally controlled the wife's finances. However, even though the husband benefited from the assets the wife brought into the marriage, they appear to have reverted back to her after his death. Also, the dowry that a wife's family paid to the husband was meant to be used for her support. On her death it didn't go to the husband or his family but rather to her progeny.

Apparently, there was a tension between the divine sanctity of marriage, cited by Jesus and based on Genesis, and the legalistic codes that defined it at the time. When Jesus railed against divorce, he seems to have been trying to cut through this complex legal construct and return to the true meaning of God's law.

Take the marriage contract itself, the *Ketubah*. It was prepared by professional scribes and was freely entered into by the husband and wife. It protected a woman by establishing exactly what the financial settlement would be if she were either widowed or divorced, an ancient pre-nuptial, in effect. However, looking at it from another perspective, it was a fine levied on a husband who divorced his wife either too quickly or without good reason. Obviously, such a document makes sense only if there was property involved. Poorer people might use more informal methods. For example, they might choose to co-habit together, giving the wife more freedom than if they were formally married. Also, there's some evidence that suggests that the poor might have used polygamy as a method of divorce. The husband simply moved in with a new wife and the old one kept her children. There is also strong reason to suggest that by the time of Jesus, women could initiate divorce. This could happen if the husband had a terrible and disfiguring disease or was engaged in a profession so disgusting, like tanning, that it made it difficult to share a home together. Finally, there was no central authority regulating the process. The Torah simply indicated that if a man was displeased with his wife, he could obtain a bill of divorce, but it did not stipulate the contents of the document itself. That would be a function of the ingenuity and legal skill of the scribe who drew it up, and this was influenced by local custom and tradition.

The demographics of marriage also suggest that fathers did not have the absolute control implied in the rabbinic texts. Most men married around thirty and their brides were normally in their late teens. In pre-modern societies women began menstruating later than today because of nutrition and other health factors. Judging by estimates of life expectancy in ancient times, most of the husbands' fathers and many of the wives' would have been already dead at the time of the marriage. Most likely, therefore, many marriages were based on mutual consent. Moreover, considering the age difference between spouses, many women would have been widowed at least once, thus acquiring a certain measure of independence. In short, all of this indicates that Jesus's world was not a static one. It was vibrant, diverse, and constantly evolving.

As we turn to daily life in first century Palestine, the physical and material environment, it becomes apparent that the Jews had many similarities with their gentile neighbors. This is reflected in their eating and dining habits. Bread was the staple of the diet, accounting for up to 50 percent of caloric intake. It was supplemented by what we would call today a healthy Mediterranean diet: olive oil and legumes, including chickpeas, lentils, and beans, were the main items on the daily menu. These were supplemented by fruits such as dates, figs, pomegranates, melons, and plums. Dairy products consisted primarily of cheeses, but some milk was produced. Fish was becoming more popular, likely under Roman influence, and it came from both the Mediterranean and the freshwater Sea of Galilee. Meat was reserved primarily for the Sabbath and religious holidays. People mostly ate lamb, but chicken, gazelle, and even deer were consumed, and surprisingly some Jews even ate pork. Wine mixed with water, as in most of the Roman Empire, was the predominant beverage. Poor transportation and spoilage ensured that most of the food consumed was locally produced, but the salting of meat and fish and drying of fruits encouraged at least some export and import.

If the basic cuisine of Jewish Palestine was not very different from that of its gentile neighbors, its dietary laws certainly set the Jews apart. However, there was no uniformity in how dietary laws were observed in different segments of Jewish society. It would be foolish to assume that rabbinic dietary restrictions recorded a century or more after the time of Jesus were uniformly observed in the early first century. Nevertheless, it is apparent that the Pharisees more strictly observed the dietary laws than their fellow Jews. This factor drove many of the confrontations between Jesus and the Pharisees, who equated strict observation of the dietary laws with ritualistic purity in the eyes of the law. This tension not only concerns relations between Jew and gentile but also among segments of the Jewish community itself.

There were two aspects of dietary law: the actual foods themselves and commensality, or the combination of various ingredients, such as the restriction on mixing meat and cheese. Many of the common people were relatively lax in their observation, even eating pork. Others, especially the Pharisees, observed the dietary laws strictly. This necessitated physical separation, especially during mealtime, resulting in a segmentation of Jewish society that limited social contact. There were also restrictions on eating with gentiles and consuming food and wine produced by them. It is probable that not every Jew observed this, but the testimony of Roman sources indicate that Jews were a people who wished to be separate. The late first century historian Tacitus remarked that Jews showed compassion for each other but since they ate and slept apart they hated other peoples. The ultimate irony is that even though Jesus and his contemporaries ate the same food and drank the same wine as their gentile neighbors, the way they did so not only separated them from non-Jews but also from many of their own people.

Food was prepared and eaten within the house, which was the center of family life. There was no typically Jewish design; houses resembled the domestic architecture, both Jewish and gentile, in the region. Except for the very rich, who could import materials, most people used local stone and wood. This could lead to some differentiation. For example, black ballast was popular in Galilee while limestone predominated in Judea. The architecture was uniform. Most people lived in a simple home with one main room and a courtyard in either the front or the rear. A "courtyard house," usually inhabited by the affluent but often shared by a few families, consisted of a few rooms surrounding a courtyard. Most houses had two stories with low ceilings. The ground floor usually had no windows, which were reserved for the second. The second story was reached either by an outdoor stone staircase or an internal wooden ladder. The two main rooms, both on the first floor, were the *traklin*, an all-purpose space used for dining, cooking, washing, and other household activities, and the *kiton*, or bedroom. There was usually one and sometimes two of these. More than that was unnecessary since multiple people slept in one bed. The *traklin* also had a communal element to it; frequently more than one family would share it. Internal partitions provided flexibility to the living spaces. The courtyard was utilized both for domestic living and as a workspace. There were also wells, drinking troughs, bath houses, and structures for animals there. The roof was also multifunctional. People ate, worked, and prayed there. It was also used for storage: fruits, vegetables, olive oil, and wine. Often rooms were added on to the house for married children and other family members. This highlights the communal nature of the living space. It was not uncommon, especially in larger villages, for shops and workshops to be attached to the outer walls.

The three major building materials were stone, wood, and soil. The walls and the foundations were made of stone bound by mortar; the ceiling, beams, and door of wood; and the floor of packed dirt. Only spaces used for storage or stabling livestock were paved. The inside of the water cisterns, filled by rain, were coated with lime. The houses of the elite resembled those of their Roman or Herodian rulers, including mosaics, polished stone, and even peristyles surrounding their courtyards, but these were not the homes that Jesus would have visited.

The clothing worn by Jews in the time of Jesus was almost the same as that worn throughout the eastern empire and bore little resemblance to the garments shown either in art or Hollywood movies. Both men and women wore tunics made from either wool or linen. They were very simple: two rectangular pieces of fabric with openings for the head and arms. The woolen ones had two vertical stripes heading down from both sides of the neck. Linen tunics were plain because of the difficulty of dying that fabric and the religious prohibition against mixing two different fabrics together. Male tunics were short, falling to the knees, while female ones reached the feet and were tied at the waist or beneath the breasts. Married women wore a second tunic over this. It had sleeves and fell to the ground. Both sexes wore a mantle over the tunic when necessary, a simple rectangle made of wool. It was not a Roman toga, but men wore it in a similar fashion, draped over the left shoulder, leaving the right hand free. Women usually attached their mantle with a brooch at the left shoulder and draped the other corner over their head. Sandals were the basic footwear and resembled modern flip flops with an ankle band thrown in.

Jewelry was not much different than that of the rest of the Mediterranean world and reflected social status. In the time of Herod the Great, people still seemed to respect the second commandment and refrained from wearing jewelry with figurative designs, but as the first century progressed this became less and less of an issue. In short, as far as clothing and jewelry went, it would have been difficult to distinguish a Jew from his gentile neighbors.

For such a complex and sophisticated society to exist, it needed an economic system to underpin it. Obviously, Palestine was not particularly rich relative to some regions of the Roman Empire. Egypt, for example, fed the city of Rome with its grain exports and Alexandria, the capital, was the empire's second city, surpassed in wealth only by Rome itself. Nevertheless, the economy of Palestine was not insignificant. Herod was extraordinarily rich and the temple that he rebuilt attracted visitors from all over the empire and beyond. Before turning to Jerusalem and its wealth, we must describe the economy of the hinterland that supported it.

The rabbinic literature written over a century after Jesus provides an idealized picture of agrarian life. The mid-sized landowners were portrayed as the backbone of society. Their holdings, under the wise and benevolent supervision of the family patriarch, were largely self-sufficient. It was a non-monetary economy underpinned by its own localized agricultural production. The wife at home focused on her domestic duties: caring for her husband and children, grinding grain to make flour, cooking, weaving wool, and perhaps supervising a domestic slave or two. The fields were tended by, and this seems to have been the case, day laborers.

As one might expect, this is not a particularly accurate description of reality. The economic and social world that Jesus inhabited was more complex than the idealized version. One example of this was that some women had more autonomy than the rabbinical sources imply. The archives of a woman named Babatha illustrate this. She lived not long after the destruction of the temple, and her archives have been found buried in the Judean desert. Relatively well off, Babatha was a widow twice over. She had inherited land from her father and, when her first husband died, he also left Babatha a large inheritance from his family business. Her second husband used her dowry to buy date orchards. However, he ran into financial difficulty and was forced to take a mortgage on a courtyard he owned in a village. On his death, the land purchased from the dowry reverted back to Babatha. Interestingly, her husband did not divorce his first wife, Miriam, who kept a separate household. In short, the rural economy reflected in these papyri was sophisticated; land, money, and loans all played their part. The Gospels also reflect such a world. Joseph was a woodworker. Peter and at least three of the other disciples were fishermen who worked on family-owned boats. The parables contain rich absentee landlords feasting while the poor suffer at their doors, affluent local ones paying day laborers, and dishonest stewards stealing from their masters and lending to financially starved tenants.

Except for the very rich, the distinction between the private and domestic space was blurred. Rooms in the home, as seen above, were divided between family life and economic production, with some used for both. Picture a courtyard with children scurrying about, the meal being prepared, laundry washed, wheat ground into flour, and wool woven into garments. Women were not confined to the home. They sold their freshly baked bread and hand-woven fabric in the marketplace. A good deal of production took place outside the home at threshing floors, olive presses, and pottery kilns. Tanning and wine making were deemed not suitable for domestic space. Even in a country village, life was more complex than a superficial assessment might suggest.

Ninety percent of the population depended on agriculture to make their living. Small and medium-sized holdings worked by their owners still existed, but as we have seen more and more parcels of land were owned by large landowners, most absentee. These estates were usually fragmented, having been acquired haphazardly over time, often by debt default. They could be leased to tenants, who paid a monetary rent, allocated to share-croppers, or worked by day laborers. Grain was the largest crop. The fields were rotated every other year and in the intervening period lentils and other soil-enriching legumes were grown. Galilee was particularly known for its olive groves, and the oil was sold locally and exported. John of Gishala, one of the leaders of the revolt, produced it on his land and made a fortune selling it to Jews living in southern Syria, who were prohibited by religious law from buying it from gentiles. Grapes were more profitable than either grain or olives. Like most of the ancient world, wine was the beverage of choice, consumed usually at a two to one water to wine ratio. Where the climate permitted there were plentiful date and fig orchards. Balsam trees were grown in the Jordan Valley. They were the source of the most valued perfume in the Roman world. Pliny wrote that balsam was worth twice its weight in silver. Originally a monopoly controlled by the Hasmoneans and then Herod, it was now an imperial one. Flax was also a very valuable crop and was used to produce linen. It grew every six years in the rotated fields. Wool was produced in both Galilee and Judea and was a valuable export.

Trade was a key component of the economy. Some items like pottery were produced and sold locally. Other commodities had a more regional market. These included wine, olive oil, dates and figs, wool, and linen. Other products, like balsam and glassware, were shipped across the Mediterranean. Lacking a network of internal waterways, goods were shipped mostly by donkey and for longer distances by camel. Both Judea and Galilee were on major trade routes from the East and there is evidence that silk from China passed through them on its way to Rome.

Despite the relative sophistication of its economy, the world of Jesus was one where most people, aside from the elites, were always in danger of falling into poverty. The situation worsened after the death of Herod, putting tremendous stress on the social fabric. Normally there was enough rain to support the crops, but it fell almost exclusively in the winter months.

Droughts occurred about every three years, often resulting in famine. The scarcity of freshwater springs exacerbated the situation. Despite relatively sophisticated agrarian methods, yields were low by modern standards and the fragmented nature of the plots didn't help. In fact, unless there was a particularly good harvest, food scarcity always plagued the countryside. Ironically, surplus grain was often stored in large walled towns and cities, so there were no reserves for the farmers who produced it. There were other constraints as well. A certain amount of the yield needed to be reserved as seed for next year's crop, making it unavailable for sale or consumption. Taxes and tithes owed to both Roman and Jewish authorities took at least half the yield off the top. Planting olives and grapes for urban consumption was a major form of income for larger landowners, but it removed valuable land from the production of food for the local population. Thus, the scarcity of land, limits to production, and the density of population resulted in social tension and often extreme poverty. No wonder there were brigands.

How did the society cope with these problems? Everyone in the family worked. The goal was to diversify the risk. Even if you owned or rented a small plot, you might also work along with your sons as a day laborer on other farms, perhaps owned by large absentee landlords. In times of severe drought rents could be adjusted. Social and religious norms encouraged this. However, there was a tension between the elites performing their charitable obligations and maintaining a luxurious urban lifestyle. Even though religious belief and social norms encouraged charity, it was limited to keeping the poor alive and nothing more. Besides that, it was a one-way street, very different from the mutual responsibilities of clients and patrons in the Greek and Roman world.

Poverty was humiliating. A poor man or woman rarely owned a mantle or wore sandals. The lack of a mantle was not only socially demeaning, but it also meant that the person lacked a cover for the night. The rich ate white bread, made from the finest grains, while slaves and the poor ate black bread. However, the impact of poverty went far beyond physical deprivation. It also had profound social implications. Access to land and its produce allowed one to live a virtuous life and observe the law. You were able to maintain the purity of your food, pay your tithes to the village synagogue, and show charity to your neighbors. You also could afford the meat, fruits, fish, eggs, and fine wines necessary for Sabbath meals and religious festivals. It allowed you to marry and arrange marriage for your children. On your death, it provided the means for a proper burial. In contrast, "people of the land," as the rural poor were called, were ignorant of the Torah and couldn't keep the law. This meant social ostracism. At its core, class structure in Jewish Palestine was not based on wealth but rather your place in the religious hierarchy. If you were socially on the bottom, what were your options? There was brigandage, of course, and many took that route. However, heading to Jerusalem to find work was perhaps a more optimal solution.

Jerusalem was located in the central highlands of Palestine, on a spur of rugged hill country running north to south from the border with Samaria to the desert of southern Judea and Idumea. From one perspective, Jerusalem was too big and too rich for the land that supported it. It was neither a port nor a trade center. The rugged hills with their ravines, steep valleys, and caverns made transportation difficult and provided lairs for the brigands. The major caravan routes bypassed Jerusalem, either running north of it just south of the Sea of Galilee or south leading from Petra to the coastal Palestinian cities and Alexandria. The primary commercial artery, used primarily for domestic trade, ran north to south. Jerusalem looked as much toward the East, where their compatriots, the Babylonian Jews, lived under Parthian rule, as it did to the hellenized port cities on the Mediterranean coast. Within Jerusalem, everything revolved around the temple, the source of its enormous prestige and wealth. It drew Jewish and gentile visitors from all over the ancient world. Arguably, it was the prime tourist destination in the Roman Empire aside from the imperial capital itself. This made the city extremely rich, but the needs of the tourists and the rich elite centered in Jerusalem siphoned off most of the produce from the hinterland. Produce was often farmed with the needs of the city and not the rural population in mind. Jerusalem was both a blessing and a curse to the greater population, but its vital importance was clear to Jews inside and outside Palestine. It was the center of the Jewish world.

Inhabited from the fourth millennium and becoming a fortress by the second, Jerusalem was conquered around 1000 BCE by King David, who made it his capital. The original inhabitants probably picked the site because of its proximity to the Gihon Spring, one of the few sources of fresh well water in the area. Eventually a tunnel was built under the city walls, connecting it to the Pool of Siloam, a rock cut reservoir, in the old City of David. It was the defensive character of the location that mattered most, making it the ideal political and religious center of first the kingdom of Israel and later the southern kingdom of Judah. The Babylonian conquest and the destruction of the First Temple was a devastating blow to the city. Even after the Persians allowed the exiles to return and rebuild the temple, Jerusalem remained a backwater situated in a minor province of an immense empire. This allowed the temple priests to dominate the affairs of the city. It was the Maccabee revolt and the foundation of the Hasmonean dynasty that changed everything; the city began to grow in area, population, and importance.

It's not easy to estimate the population of ancient Jerusalem. The inflated numbers of Josephus can certainly be dismissed. Ancient historians were notorious for choosing literary exaggeration over numerical accuracy. The best we can do today is make assumptions in respect to population density and apply them to the area of the location based on archeological excavation. The original old city, situated south of the Temple Mount with access to the Gihon Spring, had a population of about five thousand people. During the Hasmonean period the city began to grow, moving across the deep Tyropoeon Valley. The Valley of the Cheesemakers as it was called, divided the Old City from the western hills and the Mount of Zion, what would become the Upper City. This valley, running north to south past the Temple Mount, served also as Jerusalem's primary commercial artery. The population grew to more than thirty thousand in the area surrounded by the first wall. Under Herod the Great, the city grew northward, across the first wall that ran from his palace and the three towers to the Fortress Antonia and temple. This new area became another commercial district, and a second wall was added to protect it. After his death, the city continued to expand north into the suburb of Bezetha. This is where Agrippa I began to build the third wall to protect what became the New City. By the time of the great revolt, the population was approaching one hundred thousand. The influx of pilgrims during the three great festivals could multiply it by a factor of at least two or three. Both its area and population were significantly less than Rome or Alexandria, but Jerusalem stood firmly placed in the second rank of classical cities.

Even if Jerusalem was not as populous as some other major provincial centers, the presence of the largest sacred space in the empire raised its prestige to the highest level. The enormity of the temple complex, with everything needed to maintain it, had a disproportionate impact on the life of the city. The incredible number of sacrifices, both for private offerings and public festivals, required the employment of thousands of people, including priests, Levites, and a multitude of attendants. It's hard to imagine the sounds and smells of the animals being driven through the streets to the temple. The only coins permitted for the purchase of sacrificial beasts were minted in Tyre. They had a much higher level of purity than the ones produced in Antioch. This necessitated the presence of the hordes of money changers that set up their tables in the Court of the Gentiles and the Royal Stoa. It was also a public meeting place and financial center. The temple was the nerve center of the city and the entire Jewish world.

Pilgrims were constantly swarming in, especially for the three major festivals: Passover, Pentecost, and the Tabernacles. Since Pompey the Great had swept the Mediterranean of pirates a century before, sea travel was relatively easy and mostly safe. The timing of the festivals, from spring to early autumn, was ideal. It was the best time to sail; the weather was good and the seas calm. Once in Palestine, a pilgrim would find the roads dry; most of the region's rain fell in the winter. However, the journey by land, usually by foot but on donkey by the wealthy, could be dangerous. The roads were not good, far below Roman standards. The best one, improved and protected by Herod the Great, to accommodate the large community of Babylonian Jews, came from the east, crossing the Jordan at Jericho. Travelers would group together in caravans to protect themselves from the brigands who infested the Judean hills. If a traveler was particularly well known and bearing rich gifts, representatives from the temple would greet him at the gates of the city with fanfare and hordes of people, a tradition that resonates in the Gospels with the entrance of Jesus in Holy Week.

Where would people stay? A few rich pilgrims might own their own residences, but most would stay in the mansions or homes of friends or relatives or more likely in one of many inns in the city. Ordinary pilgrims would stay in hostels that catered to Jews from their home cities and synagogues. During the major feasts, though, there was simply not enough room. Families stayed in the local villages around the city or pitched tents outside the walls. One can only imagine the wealth that all these visitors brought with them. It supported the magnificence of the temple and augmented its treasury. One example of this wealth was the very vestments of the high priest, worn only while officiating at the most sacred occasions. These garments, made from the most precious fabrics and decorated with rare gems, were so valuable that the Roman prefect, like Herod and the Hasmonean kings before him, held them under his protection. This wealth provided by religious pilgrims and other visitors not only supported the temple and its staff but also flowed into the economy of the city.

As was the case in all the cities of the ancient world, rich and poor lived side by side. However, many of the great mansions inhabited by the priests and other members of the elite were on the western slope of the Upper City, facing the Temple Mount with the great palace of Herod the Great at their rear. Recent archeological excavations have uncovered a number of these, including one palatial mansion with three terraces running up the slope. It had beautifully frescoed walls and a peristyle courtyard that would rival any found in Pompey. The mansions in this area also had the ritual baths and stone and glass vessels needed to maintain ritual purity. The magnificence of these structures, and the proximity of rich and poor, are a vivid backdrop for Jesus's parable of the rich man and the beggar Lazarus.

There were magnificent houses in the Old City as well, located just south of the temple and near the eastern wall. Queen Helena of Adiabene, and other members of her family, built mansions there. Converts to Judaism, the family had close relations with the Judean elite and ruled a small client state of the Parthian Empire in northern Mesopotamia. A century later, the Greek geographer Pausanias would deem her magnificent underground tomb, located to the north outside the city walls, "a wonder to behold."

We know less about the houses of the common people. There's no evidence to suggest that they were multistory structures like the apartment blocks of Rome. Most likely they resembled the homes already described in the villages: two stories high, room to congregate on the roof and a multipurpose room for the family and sleeping space on the first floor. We might also assume that some of these had courtyards in the center and shops attached to the outside walls. Since the massive Temple Mount occupied a significant portion of the area of the city, and the ravines and valleys surrounding it allowed urban expansion only to the north, people were packed together more tightly than in most cities in the Mediterranean world. The massive inflow of pilgrims during the religious festivals made the congestion even worse.

How did the population of Jerusalem support itself? Thousands of people were employed in the temple. These included members of the great priestly families, but also the lesser ones, including the Levites and their hordes of attendants. There were also the thousands of people flooding in from the countryside, forced off their land and desperate to make a living. They composed the army of workers who completed the temple's restoration. When that project was finally completed, Herod Agrippa II put them to work on other public projects around the city to prevent social unrest. It would be wrong to imagine that all these men were unskilled. Their numbers included master stonecutters who quarried the massive blocks and cut and carved them. The great beams, along with wooden panels and roofing, made of cedar from Lebanon required skilled carpenters. Moreover, craftsmen in gold, silver, and bronze were needed to install the golden veneer and panels and mold the precious lamps, bowls, and other decorative objects that Titus would eventually carry through the streets of Rome during his triumph. Finally, all these skilled workers needed to train the priests to perform these tasks in the restricted sacred areas where they were not allowed to enter. There were also other projects available to the building trade, including the palaces and great mansions within the city and the ornate tombs for the rich outside the walls. Both skilled craftsmen and common workers were paid by the day. Interestingly, the custom was that they had to be paid for the whole day even if they only worked for a few hours, not unlike the case in the parable of the master of the vineyard.

Where would all these workers live and what was their life like? One can imagine that for many of them the standard of living resembled that of people inhabiting slums in the modern third world. Despite the squalid, densely packed, and unsanitary conditions, there was probably a sense of social cohesion beneath the surface, much like in the notorious slums of Mumbai where there is a sense of community, which is reinforced by the fact that people tend to cluster together with neighbors from their own villages in the countryside.

There were a wide range of other trades and industries in Jerusalem. First, the population needed to be fed. Olive oil was an integral ingredient of the diet. Olives were grown in the countryside, especially in the Perea region on the east bank of the Jordan, and then exported to Jerusalem where they were pressed in the northern suburbs or just outside the walls. Bread was produced in people's homes, but this did not entirely satisfy demand. There's evidence suggesting that there was a baker's bazaar in the center of the city. The butchers also had their own street, and the animals were fattened in the more sparsely populated New City. Water sellers would carry large pitchers, dispensing water to thirsty buyers; business was especially good during the hot, dry summer. The area between the first and second walls, ideally located just north of the Upper City and facing the western entrances to the temple, was the commercial center, hosting shopkeepers selling basic staples, tradesmen, and merchants. The presence of a wealthy elite and the influx of pilgrims and tourists from all over the ancient world supported a thriving market in luxury goods, where spices, ointments, and perfumes were sold. Fine glassware was locally manufactured as well as jewelry.

Class structure in Jewish Palestine was less rigid than elsewhere in the empire. Certainly, there were some occupations that were looked down upon. Gamblers, including pigeon racing trainers, herdsmen, usurers, tax collectors, publicans, and temple money changers, were all held in low repute. They had one quality in common: the ability to cheat or exploit people. Slaves were treated more humanely than in Roman and Greek society. Among other legal protections, Jewish slaves were required to be freed after six years, thus restricting their numbers. They were considered members of the household and even allowed to marry into the family after gaining freedom. If a Jewish slave was not looked down upon, gentile slaves had much lower status even if they converted and accepted circumcision. Indeed, all proselytes were considered suspect, including the Idumeans and Galileans who had been forcibly converted over a century before. Herod was a "half Jew" and a common slur was that "nothing good ever comes out of Galilee." Others who were considered to some degree suspect or even impure were illegitimate children of priests, people with physical deformities, and fatherless children. Beggars were tolerated and endemic to the city, plying their trade in public spaces and especially at the entrances of the temple. The law's injunctions respecting charity guaranteed their right to survive, if not society's responsibility to lift them from their condition.

Since religious lineage or learning, not wealth, brought status and prestige, professions in that sphere were particularly well regarded. Scribes were highly respected. Their role could entail anything from acting as a minor clerk or amanuensis to acting as an ancient notary or lawyer, but most importantly they were the chief interpreters and recorders of the law. Traditionally they were compensated for their scribal duties, but often they supported themselves with another trade. Think of Paul taking on the trade of tent maker. This reflects the opaque and less rigid nature of the Jewish social hierarchy. This quality also prevailed among the priests where religious and economic status were not necessarily aligned. The Levites who served in the temple were required to be born into the tribe of Levi. The prerequisite to become high priest, Israel's direct link to God, was descent from Aaron. The high priestly families were the closest thing to an aristocracy that existed in the Jewish world, and to protect the purity of their lineage they married only among themselves. However, this did not preclude them from making money as merchants or collecting rents as absentee landlords. Unlike Roman senators, who were expected to show some decorum in how they made money, members of the priestly class could make it however they pleased. How else could they afford their palatial mansions on the western hills of Jerusalem?

What can we conclude about the society Jesus inhabited? What did he see and experience as he traveled the dusty summer and muddy winter roads of Galilee, Judea, and beyond? He would have seen Jews who looked, dressed, and acted like the gentiles, even eating the same food and drinking the same wine as their non-Jewish neighbors, albeit with restrictions not readily apparent to the eye. Jesus would have observed a complex and often troubled social fabric with chronic tensions and divisions between city and country, rich and poor. When visiting Jerusalem, Jesus would have rubbed elbows with hellenized Jews who lived in palatial mansions as splendid as those inhabited by gentile elites in Alexandria, Antioch, and even Rome. Outside these mansions, throughout the streets and in the countryside, he would have encountered the destitute, the beggars, the handicapped, and the poorest of the poor, "the people of the land." These wouldn't have the means to lead a virtuous life by observing the law. They couldn't afford the foods to attain religious purity or pay the synagogue tithes that would make them a part of the community. Then there were the physically deformed, the illegitimate children, the tax collectors, tanners, and workers in other despised trades and the unmarried women who were considered to be second class citizens. Even Jews who had converted over a century before were looked at with suspicion. These included both the Idumeans and Galileans. Even Jesus felt the brunt of this on numerous occasions. One thing Jesus would not see much of was Romans. Rome as a power was far away. The Roman prefect was based in the gentile city of Caesarea, residing in Jerusalem only during the high holy days. His soldiers were not legionnaires but auxiliary troops recruited mostly from gentiles living in Palestine, who had no love for the Jews and vice versa: a potentially combustible combination. During Jesus's lifetime, there was no sense of national resistance to Roman oppression. If the prosperity of Jerusalem rested on the pilgrims and tourists visiting the temple, it was the Pax Romana that made it possible. In the list of social and religious problems that Jesus experienced and confronted, the issue of Roman domination would be near the bottom.

There's another element that adds a further level of complexity. I was tempted to ignore it because it just doesn't make sense. Jerusalem contained a theater for musical and theatrical performances, a hippodrome for chariot racing, and an amphitheater for gladiatorial games, all built by Herod the Great. The first two were in the confines of the Upper and Lower Cities, while the third, perhaps because of its bloodthirsty nature, stood outside the eastern wall. Who were the audiences for these public places? One doubts that a pilgrim from the Judean hills or Galilee would be sitting in the stands of any of these structures. There's not even a hint of their existence in the Gospels. Did the elites from the priestly families attend, the rich merchants or the craftsmen, the urban proletariat, gentile visitors, or Jews from the diaspora? Were these structures a function of Herod's egomania or his desire to be perceived as a Roman or Greek as well as a Jew? Most likely, our instinct to view their existence in such a sacred spot as hugely counterintuitive is a result of our modern, anachronistic mental rigidity. Is it at least possible that many residents of Jerusalem did not view this as a paradox, seeing no contradiction between being a Jew and enjoying the same spectacles as their gentile contemporaries.

Chapter 5

Religious Environment

IN ALMOST EVERY 1950s and 1960s movie spectacular about Jesus and the rise of Christianity, including my favorite, *Ben Hur*, at one point a world-weary, cynical Roman will say that all intelligent men know that the gods do not exist, that they're utter nonsense. How could anyone believe in those silly old gods, the screenwriter is implying. Besides that, such scenes paint a black and white dichotomy: unbelief, or better yet atheism, as represented by the Romans, against the good news brought by Jesus. The "good news" was certainly there, but to view the Romans or any people of the ancient world as atheists is simply anachronistic. It's seeing their world through our own eyes. As the eminent British historian Keith Hopkins observed, the world that Jesus lived in was "a world full of gods."

"A world full of gods": what does that really mean? Hopkins is not referring to institutional or official religion represented by the pantheon of Roman and Greek gods. Worshiping the gods of your city was a sign of political loyalty and social cohesion, a civic duty not a religious one. It was used as an instrument of political control. Emperor worship also fell into this category. It was a loyalty test. If a Christian refused to worship a statue of the emperor, it was not perceived as a religious act but a dangerous political statement. Religious tolerance was the norm in the Roman world, but not in our modern sense of the word. It was based on the two fundamental attributes that almost all the religions of the ancient world, excepting of course Judaism and Christianity, exhibited: syncretism and lack of exclusivity. The first refers to the belief that the gods are interchangeable; the

Greek Zeus is the same as the Roman Jupiter, Aphrodite as Venus, and so on. The second is the notion that a person can worship different gods and hold more than one set of beliefs simultaneously. As the historian Morton Smith points out, ancient peoples had no notion of the word "religion" in the way we use it today.

Beneath the surface of institutionalized civic religion, however, supernatural belief in its many forms—gods, spirits, demons, magic—permeated every corner of society. The cities of the Roman Empire were dotted with temples; there were altars at the crossroads and statues of the gods everywhere. Superstition was the norm. For example, before making an important decision, such as going into battle, a Roman general would consult an auger, who used techniques handed down from the Etruscans. He consulted the organs of a slaughtered animal to confirm that the timing was propitious. Every home had its household gods, the Lares and Penates, which were worshiped in their miniature shrine. Even the origin of the gladiatorial games was religious, originally performed at the funerals of the elite. To believe that ancient peoples could be anything but religious and superstitious results from viewing them through our own secular lenses.

Mystery religions complimented the civic pantheon. These cults dealt with issues that have always fascinated humans: death and the prospect of an afterlife. Roman legionnaires brought the cult of Mithras back from the East and it quickly spread across the western empire. Originating in Persia, its central tenant revolved around a Zoroastrian myth concerning the god Mithras, usually depicted killing a bull or riding his chariot to the sun. The exact meaning behind the myth is unclear, probably because of the secrecy in the cult that shrouded it. Membership was limited to males, and meetings, mostly in the form of banquets, were conducted in secret underground vaulted spaces. There was an initiation ceremony, various grades of membership, and even a secret handshake, sort of an ancient Masonic lodge. The nebulous nature of its underlying precepts allowed, even encouraged, participation in the civic religion and even other mystery religions. Another cult, or "insider religion," was the Eleusinian Mysteries. Based on the myth of Demeter and Persephone, it revolved around the notions of rebirth and the afterlife; the initiates, for a price, were able to participate in rituals that evoked these states. The cult of Isis, like the Eleusinian Mysteries, also had a long history. She was an ancient Egyptian goddess who represented fertility, both feminine and agricultural, and the protection of seafarers. Her worship spread throughout the Mediterranean and merged into both Greek and Roman religion. Like the other cults, the followers of Isis formed a community of kindred spirits, forged by direct participation in the rites or as spectators.

Throughout the empire, therefore, religion in all its various forms permeated the cultural consciousness. Although it influenced every aspect of people's lives, the undogmatic, syncretic, and nonexclusive nature of pagan religion made it very different from its modern counterpart. It also explains why pagans found the exclusivity and dogmatic nature of Judaism and Christianity to be alien and even threatening. Indeed, there was an underlying tension between the Jews and their gentile neighbors. To Jesus and his fellow Jews, pagan beliefs surrounded them in their own land, even if they didn't impact their immediate lives. Invisible barriers, including strict adhesion to the law, protected them. Torah, covenant, and temple separated Jews from their gentile neighbors. Still, it wasn't all cut and dry; the differences with pagan religion were certainly fundamental and profound, but there were also some surprising similarities.

Josephus is our starting point for understanding Judaism at the time of Jesus. He doesn't even attempt to explain the core of Judaism at the time, temple and Torah, or even discuss the radical notion of monotheism itself. Josephus instead moves immediately to the periphery, the various Jewish sects. "Among the Jews," he writes, "there are three schools of thought, the Pharisees, Sadducee and Essenes." This classification is certainly an oversimplification. First, they are sects and represent a minority of the Jewish population. He gives the most space to the Essenes, who, although respected for their extreme piety, operated on the margins of society. Josephus also removes all the fluidity, complexity, and nuance from the equation, oversimplifying the distinctions. However, Josephus was writing in Greek for a gentile audience, attempting to explain Judaism in a way they could relate to. This audience explains the disproportionate space he gives the Essenes. His readers, totally familiar as they were with the pagan mystery cults, would find his description of the Essenes' customs assessable, representing exemplary virtue, but they would also be intrigued by what was simply "a great read."

But let's start our discussion with the Pharisees. They have suffered from a bad press in the Gospels and even Josephus. He recognizes their virtues and respects them for standing up to authority, but mostly views them as annoying troublemakers. In the Gospels, along with the scribes, the Pharisees are depicted as Jesus's rhetorical antagonists, wanting to depict him as a bad Jew without respect for the law. They serve as Jesus's "straight men"; their hypocrisy and stupidity set again his love, insight, and compassion. He makes the Pharisees' attitude toward the law appear petty, mere nitpicking. The Pharisees are out to get Jesus at every opportunity.

This depiction, however, is one dimensional and unfair. Even Josephus admits that the Pharisees are "held to be the most authoritative exponents of the law and count as the leading sect." He points out that even though the Pharisees accept that men have responsibility for their own choices, "they ascribe everything to fate or to God." Souls are imperishable; those of the good pass into other bodies while the souls of the bad are "subjected to eternal punishment." Josephus compares them to the Sadducees, who believe in free will, and denied the permanence of the soul. The Sadducees' beliefs are also recorded in the New Testament. In Mark, Jesus debates the Sadducees at the temple over resurrection. And Paul, as recorded in Acts, cleverly provoked an argument over the question of resurrection between the Pharisees and Sadducees to disrupt his trial before the high priest. If the Pharisees of the Scriptures come across as petty and vindictive, the Sadducees are portrayed as truly sinister.

Josephus provides further insight into both groups. While he paints the Sadducees as boorish and rude to both their peers and social inferiors, the Pharisees are affectionate toward each other, cultivate harmony in the community, and show deference to their elders. They embrace simplicity and avoid an ostentatious lifestyle. The Sadducees, on the other hand, came mainly from the elite, representing the high priestly class and heredity status. The Pharisees did not come from one class. Some were members of the elite, even sitting on the Sanhedrin, but it was their learning and observation of the law that defined them. They did not confine themselves to the Torah, like the Sadducees, in interpreting the law. They considered the customs of their ancestors in analyzing the logic of the doctrine that stood behind it. Their knowledge of the law evoked respect from the community, even from those who did not observe it rigidly. (The word *Pharisee* itself is derived from Hebrew and Aramaic, meaning "separate ones" and "interpreters.") This provided them with influence and popularity in the community that the Sadducees, centered in Jerusalem, could never achieve.

According to Josephus, during the Hasmonean period the Pharisees were a significant political force. They upheld Jewish tradition in the face of the Hellenism infecting the Hasmonean elites. During the reign of John

Hyrcanus (134 to 104 BCE), they possessed a great deal of influence at court. It was not to last.

King Hyrcanus asked the Pharisees during a banquet if he was doing anything wrong as a ruler. Naturally they said no and went on to praise him effusively. However, a man named Eleazar interrupted to everyone's astonishment and begged to differ. Hyrcanus should step down as high priest, he argued, because his mother had once been a captive, an explosive remark that implied that she had been sexually violated, making the king impure. The high priesthood was the cornerstone of Hyrcanus's royal legitimacy, so naturally he was incensed. A close friend of the king, a Sadducee named Jonathan, saw this as an opportunity to undermine his political rivals. He suggested that the Pharisees were really the ones behind Eleazar's accusation even though they professed outrage at the remarks. As a test of their loyalty, Jonathan demanded that they propose a penalty for Eleazar. Jonathan knew that the Pharisees interpreted the law liberally and opposed capital punishment. When the Pharisees did what Jonathan expected and didn't propose execution as a verdict, Hyrcanus perceived it as gross disloyalty and dismissed them from the royal entourage. Except for a brief revival under Queen Alexandra, this marked the end of their political power. They would oppose King Herod on matters of principle, but by the time of Jesus one could not categorize them as a political party or even a faction. Some Pharisees would play prominent roles in the great revolt but as individuals, not representing the sect.

This vivid, entertaining story might or might not be true. What's important to us is the insight it provides into how the Pharisees interpreted the law. The Sadducees, basing their concept of the law on a strict originalist reading of the Torah, took a minimalist approach that didn't mitigate its severity. The Pharisees' utilization of custom and precedence resulted in a natural evolution leading toward a greater leniency that reflected the needs of society. This enhanced their popularity. However, as reasonable as this approach to the law might appear to us, it was not only the Sadducees who took issue with it. Texts in the Dead Sea Scrolls, found in the Essene community at Qumran, refer to the Pharisees as "seekers of smooth things," alluding to the belief that they were too accommodating, twisting the law to suit their own beliefs.

The description of the Pharisees in the Gospels and the early rabbinic texts provide a different perspective. They appear to be more concerned with the technicalities of the law rather than its true meaning. It could be argued that Mark gives the most authentic portrayal of the Pharisees in the time of Jesus. It was written first, around 70 CE, and describes them as they were before the destruction of the temple. Matthew, Luke, and John wrote after this cataclysmic event and tend to reflect the new world in which the Pharisees operated, one lacking the influential temple priests.

Mark usually bunches the Pharisees and the scribes together in his narration, pitting both against Jesus. Although the two groups are not synonymous, there is overlap. Pharisees represented a voluntary association of like-minded individuals from all classes and professions, in effect a religious and social interest group. They were mostly concentrated in Judea and represented about 10 to 20 percent of the adult male population. The scribes were members of a profession. Their status was based on their ability to read and write in Hebrew, Aramaic, and in many cases Greek. At the lower rung were the scribes who wrote letters or prepared legal documents for the illiterate masses. The profession also included scribes employed in the temple or who served as government officials. At the apex of this hierarchy were the highly respected interpreters of the religious and secular law. These were the men Jesus despised: the hypocrites in long robes who took the best seats in the synagogue. A Pharisee could be a scribe, of course, but it was not a requirement for the job. Likewise, a Pharisee could be a temple priest, but a priest did not need to be a Pharisee.

What were Jesus and the Pharisees fighting over in Mark? They certainly were not disputing theological issues, such as life after death, free will or fate, but rather what appears, on the surface at least, to be technical issues of the law, including tithing, ritual purity, and the Sabbath. Jesus never denied or even challenged the legitimacy of the Torah but searched for its deeper meaning, or what we would call today its original intent. The conflict was fundamentally over social control. The Pharisees perceived themselves as the pillars of the community, defending it against an upstart Galilean from a lower-class artisan family.

One such incident occurred when the Pharisees observed the disciples "plucking grain" as they passed through a field on the Sabbath. The issue was not theft. The Torah allows poor people to pluck pieces of grain or pick grapes from a landowner's field or vineyards, if they didn't use a sickle or carry a basket. The issue in the eyes of the Pharisees was the Torah's injunction to keep the Sabbath. Jesus was not arguing against its sanctity; rather he was making a legal argument against the Pharisees' interpretation of the law. He viewed the Sabbath as a gift from God, representing a humanitarian obligation to provide a day of rest for everyone, including servants and slaves. It wasn't intended to prevent those who were poor or hungry from gaining sustenance. In another example, the Pharisees berate the disciples for not washing their hands before eating. This had nothing to do with our modern views of cleanliness, but rather represented an obsessive fear of ritual impurity. Again, Jesus was not arguing against keeping the law but pointing out that too much emphasis on the technicalities of ritual purity detracts from the more serious matter of moral purity.

The tone of Mark, and that of the other Gospels, implies repeatedly that the Pharisees were focused on trivial technical issues. This viewpoint is reinforced when we look at the early rabbinic texts. These include the earliest writings of the Mishnah from about 200 CE and the Tosefta, a commentary composed about a century later. The rabbis perceived the Pharisees as their predecessors and their teachings as precedent. However, they also focus on what appear to be arcane legal disputes.

Perhaps the most influential Pharisee in the eyes of the early rabbis was Hillel the Elder. Born in Babylon, he lived in Jerusalem during the time of Herod the Great. Hillel supported himself as a woodcutter but dedicated his life to the study of the Torah. On a certain level, he personified the transition of the Pharisees from an active political faction into a more passive social and intellectual force. Rather than political influence, their priority became interpreting the law. One example of using oral tradition to adjust the Torah was the *prosbul*, the legal construct that superseded the cancelation of debt in the Sabbatical Year. This helped society, in the eyes of Hillel and his followers, since there would otherwise be no incentive for creditors to lend to those in need of funds. Simon Ben Gamaliel, reputed to have been a teacher of Paul, was a descendant of Hillel and also a major influence on rabbinic tradition.

We know little about the actual lives of these sages, but the issues discussed in the rabbinic texts reflect those narrated in the Gospels. They seem to be overly legalistic and often abstruse, concerned mostly with ritual purity, observation of dietary laws, which included farming and harvesting, and keeping the Sabbath. Indeed, the form and mnemonic patterns of the pericopes (the term scholars give to the story or extract from a religious text often based on oral tradition) in both the Mishnah and the Gospels resemble each other. However, the legalistic, almost trivial, hairsplitting depicted in the rabbinical texts often hid deeper philosophical meaning. One example from the Mishnah recounts a dispute between the House of

Shammai and the House of Hillel. It deals with the issue of cleanliness in respect to ordinary food. At what point does the liquid honey in a honeycomb become susceptible to uncleanliness? The followers of Shammai argued that it was the point when the bees are smoked out of the hive, but those of Hillel asserted that it only became unclean when it was broken open and the honey scooped out. To anyone outside Pharisaic and rabbinic circles this would be seen as trivial nitpicking. Nevertheless, it was actually a discussion of an important philosophical issue that was being framed in concrete terms. Shammai's school was arguing that a secondary cause, the intention to eventually use honey, is the trigger. Hillel's followers rejected this interpretation. Intentionality is not enough; the actual action itself must be judged. Considering an act is not the same as doing it. This had important ethical implications.

So, who were the Pharisees? Did they reflect a political or philosophical movement as depicted by Josephus? Were they the nitpicking hypocrites that the Gospels portray? Or were they a table fellowship making rules separating themselves from society? What makes it difficult to define them today is the biases embedded in the sources. Not only was Josephus writing for a non-Jewish audience, but he had also politically opposed the Pharisees during the revolt. Nevertheless, the theological beliefs he ascribes to them were real. For example, there is archaeological evidence supporting the notion that they believed in resurrection around the time of Jesus. Excavation of the tombs from that period indicate that there often was a secondary burial, when the body was reburied in an ossuary, based on a belief in resurrection. Archaeological artifacts also confirm the existence of dietary rules and ritual bathing. Even the design of synagogues, some scholars suggest, indicate a strong Pharisaic influence.

Still, the Gospels rarely put the Pharisees in a good light. They're viewed as being so wrapped up in legalism that they miss the moral and ethical underpinning of the law. Criticism of the Pharisee's misuse of the law, moreover, is not limited to the Gospels. The Dead Sea Scrolls criticized their use of custom and tradition to supplement the Torah. Moreover, we must also not lose sight of the fact that the Gospels were written more than half a century after the death of Jesus and, except for Mark, following the destruction of the temple. It is highly probable that the negative portrait of them reflects struggles within the early church. Some Christians were undoubtedly Pharisees, or closely related to them, and reflected positions, such as the need to be circumcised before conversion, that opposed the views expounded by the writers of the Gospels.

The characterization of the Pharisees in the Mishnah is much more positive in tone. This is not surprising. The rabbis viewed themselves as coming from that tradition. Nevertheless, the emphasis on following the law more strictly than others reinforces the notion that they were an insular sect with little influence outside of its boundaries. However, this is a misconception. It was not that they were unconcerned with larger issues or ignored the broader law: marriage, divorce, property, or even criminal litigation. Rather, the Pharisees focused on dietary issues, ritual purity, and the Sabbath because that was what set them apart, made them special. Table fellowship provided them with an identity. They believed that it was important to take ritual purity of the temple and apply it to everyday life. They were not so much separating themselves from society as setting themselves up as a positive example. As we shall see, this was a very different approach from that of the Essenes. Therefore, the Pharisees needed to define carefully the laws that defined them. Their way of life also provided them with respect from the community. If no longer a political force, the Pharisees were certainly a moral one in their own communities. Finally, despite their negative press, the Pharisees had a positive impact on Jewish life and thought. Sticking solely to the written Torah as a source for law would have resulted in an antiquated and inflexible legal system. Developing what was in effect a "common law" supplementing the Torah brought life and vibrancy to social institutions. If the technical, legalistic arguments in the Gospels and Mishnah erected social boundaries, the Pharisees' more liberal approach to the law led to legal innovations in marriage and divorce, credit and debt, and even criminal procedure with an evolution toward greater leniency. As Josephus observed, besides being more pious than others, the Pharisees interpreted the laws more accurately. Beyond piety, there also was also a vibrant spiritual element in their thinking, especially their focus on the afterlife and the role of fate. As the archaeological evidence indicates, the idea of resurrection was in the air at the time of Jesus. Moreover, the Pharisees used the law to define Jewish identity and protect it from the cultural diversity that surrounded it. Within these protective barriers a richer Judaism could exist, where such vital concepts as the afterlife could be developed and nurtured.

Despite their innovative quality and prestige, the Pharisees did not question the central tenets of Judaism. Worship was centralized at the temple and controlled by a hereditary elite of priestly families. The temple cult represented the central ideology of the nation. Its cornerstone was the Torah and the covenant, the constitution of the Jewish people. Josephus declared that what God gave Moses in the form of the Torah was "a happy life and orderly constitution." However, the Torah's final compilation came much later than we would imagine, and it certainly was not written by Moses.

Judaism evolved into its unique form of monotheism over many centuries, but, like other ancient religions at that time, it still possessed syncretic elements, including a merging together of local deities. This syncretic tendency never completely disappeared, even by the time of Jesus, especially in areas recently converted by the Hasmoneans. Costobar, a brother-in-law of Herod the Great, for example, considered himself a Jew but still worshiped his Idumean ancestral god Qos. Indeed, polytheism was endemic throughout Jewish history, especially in the centuries before the Babylonian exile. Yahweh was the first among the gods, already possessing a uniqueness not shared by pagan deities, but not the only God in Israel and Judah. The prophets frequently railed against these other gods. Around 700 BCE, King Hezekiah of the southern kingdom of Judah cleansed the temple, broke the idols, and destroyed the "high places," where people could sacrifice to God outside of Jerusalem. His son Manasseh, on the other hand, rebuilt the high places, set up a statue of the goddess Asherah, claimed by some to be the wife of Yahweh, and allowed pagan idols in the temple precincts. Later Josiah, a reformer like his grandfather Hezekiah, removed the images of the goddess from the temple and destroyed the high places. Even Yahweh, the God of the Jews, displayed anthropomorphic attributes: talking, walking, and possessing feelings. In order to understand the religious world of Jesus, where the official religion centered on Torah, covenant, and the temple, it is necessary to understand the evolution of the Jewish Bible and the various strands of thought that composed it.

The final form of the Torah (Pentateuch or "five scrolls" in Greek) is a product of the fifth century BCE, assembled after the return from the Babylonian exile. It contains several strands, each reflecting a particular and often contradictory viewpoint, originating at various times and places. The custom in biblical scholarship is to categorize texts and sources by letter. For example, the earliest texts have been named "J" and "E." These were based on oral tradition and were probably written sometime in the eighth century BCE. One scholar, John Barton, characterizes them as representing the "saga" tradition. They tell their stories vividly and often violently, with heroes and villains, resembling other early traditional narratives, like the *Iliad, Odyssey,* and the Icelandic sagas. J is named after Yahweh (the German "J" is pronounced as a "Y") and was written in the southern kingdom of Judah. God was always referred to as Yahweh and the patriarchs outshine Moses. Yahweh is often anthropomorphically represented, showing human characteristics. As for E, it stands for El or Elohim, the name of the local ancient Canaanite deity. Written in the northern kingdom of Israel, God is referred to as Elohim until he reveals his name to Moses at the burning bush. Moses has precedence in the narrative. The writers of E, although they originated in the Northern Kingdom, opposed the religious establishments of both Israel and Judah, where both insisted that only the descendants of Aaron, Moses's older brother, were qualified for the high priesthood. To the authors of E, the golden calf was anathema. It was a symbol of El, the bull god of Canaan. Also, to their great consternation, it was represented on the throne of the kings of Israel in the Northern Kingdom. The depiction of Aaron erecting the idol of the golden calf, while Moses was receiving the tablets of the Ten Commandments on Mount Sinai, is dramatic and disturbing, a searing indictment of his line's right to the high priesthood. On the other hand, the J writers magnified the role of Aaron and tended to diminish Moses. After the destruction of the Northern Kingdom by the Assyrians in 722 BCE, the Torah written by the authors of E was carried to Jerusalem, the capital of Judah. It was combined with J to form one continuous, if at times contradictory, narrative. Since both texts were derived from the same oral tradition imbued with a common communal memory, it would have been impossible to suppress either of them. Furthermore, the existence of two competing texts would have diminished the authority of both. This tendency to intermingle competing strands would continue in the evolution of the Old Testament.

The Deuteronomic source (D) has many similarities to E, leading scholars to believe that it also was derived from the tradition of the Levite priests at Shiloh in the Northern Kingdom, who migrated south to the kingdom of Judah. These similarities mostly revolve around their depiction of Moses. Not only considered a good and godly man, Moses is the central character of the whole story. Deuteronomy, the fifth book of the Torah, was probably compiled in the late seventh century. Many scholars believe that it was the scroll discovered in 622 BCE by the high priest in the temple during the reign of King Josiah. Unlike the other books of the Torah that were woven together from the J and E narratives, it is mostly a distinct work coming from one source. Deuteronomy not only completed the Pentateuch, but it also added a whole new dimension to Judaism.

Deuteronomy recounts Moses's farewell address to his people. He urges them to be faithful to God, the source of divine blessing and all human happiness. However, Deuteronomy has a deeper agenda, reflecting the push for religious reform during King Josiah's reign. It recapitulates the Ten Commandments and the law, often more humanely. Further, it bans the worship of all other gods and decrees that worship be centralized at one location, the temple. God becomes more abstract and cosmic. He does not personally inhabit the temple. The ark is not literally his footstool. This did not depict the world of Moses, where Yahweh remained anthropomorphic and other gods existed. It reflects instead a Judaism much closer to that which Jesus would have known, centered on Torah and temple. The movement toward centralization of sacrifice and worship was a pragmatic way to impose monotheism on a population that still had an attraction to local deities.

The influence of D was not limited to the book of Deuteronomy. The books of the Old Testament from Joshua to Kings, a narrative of the history of the Jewish people from the death of Moses to the final fall of the Southern Kingdom in 587 BC and the destruction of the First Temple, were drawn together, or redacted, by the D source. By redaction we mean a recompilation, editing or altering, and organization of sources that already exist. The constant theme of the Deuteronomistic historian revolves around the relationship of the people of Israel with their unique God, Yahweh. It recounts the conquest of Canaan by the Israelites, the wild west days of Judges with the stories of heroes like Samson and Gideon, the unification of the nation under the kings, the breakup into two separate kingdoms, and finally the destruction of them both. The entire narrative centers on King David. His portrait in the books of Samuel and the beginning of Kings is perhaps the most vivid and psychologically nuanced biography of anyone in ancient literature. Again and again, faithfulness to Yahweh is stressed, along with highlighting the importance of the Torah and the temple. A subtle but critical change is made in the perception of the covenant between God and people. The covenant is now between Yahweh and the line of David instead of Abraham or Moses. When the covenant is respected, peace and prosperity reign; if broken, disaster ensues.

The reign of King Josiah represented the pinnacle of the Deuteronomist's narrative: the centralization of worship in the temple, representing faithfulness to Yahweh and the institutionalizing of monotheism. However, shortly after Josiah's death, Judah was conquered by the Babylonians, the temple destroyed, and the line of David extinguished. What did this do to the covenant? Was it still valid? D, or what some scholars term D2, solved the problem. The faithless Jewish people got what they deserved. The covenant, however, still existed, but not in relation to any current occupant of the throne, but rather to a future one from the line of David who would save his people: a messiah. This explains why it was so important for a resident of Galilee to be born in Bethlehem to establish his Davidic bona fides.

One outcome of the conquest of Judah was the exile of at least a part of the population to Babylon. This fostered the idea that God could no longer be perceived as local; he needed to be universal. The temple was destroyed, the ark had disappeared forever, and the line of David was extinguished. This is where the last strand of the Jewish Bible comes into play, the Priestly one or P. The Priestly text chronologically followed J and E, but there is some academic controversy over when it was written. Some scholars have set the date very late, perhaps even after the return from exile in the late sixth century. Others believe P was composed as early as the reign of King Hezekiah in the late eighth or early seventh century BCE. What we do know is that it was merged into the other strands after the return from exile.

In 458 BCE, King Artaxerxes of Persia sent Ezra, a scribe and priest from the line of Aaron, back to Jerusalem with a letter authorizing him to teach and "enforce the law of your God." Using this authority, including the death penalty, he implemented reforms, notably strict observation of the Sabbath and the dissolution of marriages between Jews and non-Jews. With the support of the governor, Nehemiah, Ezra ordered the walls of Jerusalem rebuilt. But most importantly, he brought home the full Torah and had it read to the people. It was a new and improved version, never heard before, with the Priestly strand woven in. We don't know if Ezra was the actual author or redactor, but he was certainly intimately involved in the process.

Ezra was descended from Aaron and represented the Priestly tradition. Why didn't he just leave out the earlier strands? The answer is obvious. By that time the belief that Moses was the author of Torah was firmly entrenched in the psyche of the nation. The old stories and traditions could not be erased. The Priestly text, therefore, was interwoven into the narrative, and sometimes a second version of the same story was simply added. The beginning of Genesis is a prime example of the skill of the redactor. The first chapter of Genesis presents creation as a cosmic event described in a stately, impersonal priestly style that highlights the celestial grandeur of the event. Then in the second chapter we get a second account. It appears to shift from the general to the specific, from the heavens to the earth, but it's a separate story with an altered timeline and a different presentation of God. As Genesis continues the earlier J strand becomes more pronounced. The description of the fall, Adam and Eve's expulsion from the garden of Eden, takes on all the attributes of the "saga" narrative style. Adam and Eve are real people, God is anthropomorphic, the serpent talks, and cherubs exist. Later in Genesis the redactor added a more cosmic priestly rendition of the flood and weaves it into the earlier narrative to make one story. In the case of Deuteronomy, he kept the continuity of the story intact simply by rearranging the accounts of Moses's death from the various strands. These are just a few examples of the amazing feat accomplished by the redactor. Rather than attempting to put P in direct opposition to the other traditions, he interwove it into the narrative, subtly changing its tone and solidifying the priestly concept of God and the law. The redactor, as the biblical scholar Richard Elliot Friedman points out, accomplished something incredible. He combined the transcendent God of P with the personal Gods of J, E, and D and the whole became greater than the parts. God is cosmic in the highest sense of the word, but he cares about us. He's real.

The Torah carried by Ezra to Jerusalem was the final component of the Judaism that existed in the time of Jesus. The temple was rebuilt, allowing the centralization process to continue, and sacrifice could only take place there. With the absence of a legitimate king, the high priest held the highest authority, and the requirement that he be from the line of Aaron was retained. The notion that the priests were the only legitimate intermediary between God and man was firmly entrenched. The completed Torah became the foundation of the law. While J, E, and D frequently mentioned God's mercy, P excluded that quality, focusing instead on justice. The tension between justice and mercy, however, never disappeared, and it takes on a profound relevance in the Gospels. The trend making God less human and more cosmic was reinforced by the integration of the P text into the narrative. This was augmented during Babylonian exile by God's evolution from a local to a universal deity, not confined to the land of the Jews. This retreat from anthropomorphism also explains why the Sadducees, who represented the priestly elite, rejected the notion of angels and life after death. Angels did not square with the Priestly perception of a cosmic God. Resurrection, for its part, was simply not in the Torah. The richness of

Judaism, however, came from the complex nature of all its traditions. Not only did the Hebrew scriptures recount vividly the history of its people in a rich literary style; they also developed a profound concept of God, both celestial and accessible. Beyond that, the Torah explained how to serve and worship him. Judaism stood on a firm foundation, centered on the temple and ruled by the Torah: one God, one temple, one law.

The redactor both enriched the theology of Judaism and ensured the power of the temple elite. The political system, supported by foreign rulers, whether Persian, Hellenistic, or Roman, was theocratic, ruled by priests; its ideology was the Torah, the law code that formed the constitution of the Jews living in Palestine. The high priest, the mediator between Israel and God, and his council served as the final interpreter of the law. Everything centered on the temple; synagogues were meeting places, not sacred spaces. The temple was the symbol of the Jewish nation, and its cult was hugely popular. Why else would a large Idumean force, recent converts to Judaism, join a largely hopeless revolt to protect it?

This ideology, centering on God, Torah, and the temple was deceptively simple. God gave the Jewish people the Torah, which celebrated their national epic and defined their constitution, offering a contract or covenant with God. Observe the law, be faithful to God, and he will protect you. This constitution was unique in the ancient world. Perhaps most importantly, it was remarkably egalitarian. All Jews were held to the same standards and were treated accordingly. Observation of the law was the sole requirement. Certainly, there was a tension between an hereditary priesthood and individual equality, but on the whole social conflict was avoided. There was room for negotiation and compromise. The Pharisees represented people from all walks of life, but, while accepting the core ideology, they expanded the definition of the law. However, there was a deeper, more profound issue. By stripping Judaism down to its bare bones, de-emphasizing the mystery and myth, and turning it into a straightforward deal with God, where keeping the law was challenging but possible, a disturbing paradox emerged. The reward promised for keeping the covenant was an orderly world ruled by a just God. But what if the world was not orderly, but chaotic, with injustice and evil everywhere? How do you explain it and, even more importantly, cope with it? As an eminent scholar of the Dead Sea Scrolls puts it: "Why did the righteous continue to suffer and the wicked to prosper in a world governed by the one true God?" The priests saw the temple as the direct link to the divine, the symbolic entrance to the upper world, but this didn't adequately deal with these very human concerns.

There were ways to confront the issue. One could ostentatiously remove oneself from society to show a profound pietism. Josephus writes that as a young man he spent three years in the desert seeking spiritual enlightenment with a hermit named Bannus, who lived off the land and wore clothing made only from unwoven natural fabric. Most likely this was an exaggeration for the consumption of a gentile audience, but it highlights the respect shown to those seeking purity through extreme social segregation.

John the Baptist, consuming locusts and wild honey and wearing clothing made from camel hair fastened by a leather belt, was part of this tradition. Josephus also speaks of what he calls the Fourth Philosophy, founded by a brigand and rebel named Judas of Galilee, which accepted only the rule of God. People might turn to magic: exegesis, the interpretation of divine texts, the use of amulets or magical papyri, or even employing, as they did in Idumea, incantation texts bearing the names of the old gods to control demons, often represented by bad minor deities. Many of the old Canaanite deities were retained, albeit demoted to demonic status.

This was not, however, a systematic solution to this existential problem, and in some instances these remedies represented the traditional popular beliefs and old gods that the centralization of temple and Torah were meant to suppress. The solution? To incorporate myth into the system of belief, harnessing it to address the paradoxes the official temple ideology could not address. Not everyone was in favor of this. The Sadducees refused to believe in either angels or the afterlife. Nevertheless, many in the elite, including priests, scribes, and Pharisees, not only found these myths to be attractive but also coopted them to ease the tension between the official religion and popular beliefs, reconciling the existence of evil with a good and just God. This was not meant to replace the temple and the Torah or supersede the covenant. The scribes and priests who interpreted the law also promulgated the myths. The result was a richer multidimensional religion that often eased social and religious tension.

The myth was both apocalyptic, looking toward the end of the world, and eschatological, focusing on the resurrection of the body, the final judgment, and the afterlife. Obviously based on older localized oral tradition, it was articulated in non-canonical books written during the intertestamental period; that is, the time between the completion of the Old Testament in the fourth century BCE and the writing of the New Testament in the first century CE. One of the most important of these, the first book of Enoch, was written sporadically during that period. A minor figure mentioned in Genesis, Enoch is taken on earthly and heavenly journeys and is taught the secrets of the universe. He witnesses apocalypses and views the final judgment. According to this text, God creates the universe, but then evil subdeities seize control of creation. God retreats to a splendid higher heaven while history plays out; Satan in turn controls the earth. There is a struggle between good and evil, hints of a messianic figure, and eventually God is the victor. The righteous are rewarded and the evil punished. The book of Enoch describes a world very different from the temple and Torah ideology. It's a chaotic one; we don't get what we deserve; humans are victims controlled by fate. Although the language is monotheistic, moral dualism and polytheism permeate it. Remarkably, Enoch was composed not long after the Priestly redactor finalized the Torah.

Torah and myth ultimately complement each other. God intentionally allowed himself to be defeated; it was all part of a bigger predetermined plan. The Torah provides the law, which ensures social stability on earth while providing guidelines on how to be righteous in the eyes of God. The myth explains chaos and evil and offers hope in the afterlife for the righteous. The covenant and the law tell you what to eat, regulate marriage, and teach how to worship. The myth explains what went wrong, how to use magic to cure the sick and protect us from our enemies, and promises us that things will change. Therefore, popular beliefs, including demons, astrology, and even the old Canaanite gods, were tolerated. Rather than fighting myth as heresy, the temple elite coopted it and integrated it into Judaism. Many of these themes survived in the gnostic texts that were excluded from the canon of the New Testament. Beliefs do not die easily.

This lack of religious conformity encouraged the development of sects. The Sadducees were the most conservative, focused on the law and Torah. The Pharisees expanded the law and believed in both an afterlife and angels. However, the Essenes were the most extreme, incorporating ostentatious separation, the acceptance of apocalyptic and eschatological myth, and a thorough rejection of the temple cult. Part of this resentment was based on their rejection of wealth and property. The temple had a bloated bureaucracy and supported a wealthy and often idle elite. However, it ran much deeper. It was based on the Essenes' own founding myth, one with some basis in history.

In 153 BCE, Jonathan Apphus, who took over leadership of the Maccabee revolt after the death of his brother Judas, was appointed high priest by the Seleucid pretender Alexander, who would soon defeat his rival Demetrius for the throne. This solidified Jonathan's power and strengthened the legitimacy of the Hasmonean dynasty. However, many people did not accept this. Since the construction of King Solomon's Temple and the installation of its high priest, Zadok, the office of high priest was restricted to the line of Aaron. The Maccabees clearly didn't meet this requirement, and in the eyes of many Jews this was sacrilege. The Essenes believed that the Zadokian priest who was replaced by Jonathan was the founder of their sect. He was the "Teacher of Righteousness," who left Jerusalem for the desert. Jonathan in turn was vilified as the "Wicked Priest." From that time on members of this new sect refused to worship at the temple. It was impure for two reasons: the high priest did not descend from Aaron, and the law, or "halakah," was not followed strictly. Moreover, the Righteous Teacher believed that the calendar, which was used for setting the holy days and festivals, was imprecise since it was not based on a 364-day solar year. The actual history is unclear but much of it rings true. The Jews were in revolt against the Seleucids. The high priests had lost prestige because of their repeated failure to resist hellenization, making it easier to replace them. The Hasmoneans made the high priesthood the foundation of their legitimacy, but this tarnished their reputation as national saviors among many of the devout. On top of this, a series of extraordinary archeological discoveries in the late 1940s and early 1950s not only provided a location, Qumran, where the sect might have first established itself, but also revealed a series of documents that have revolutionized biblical scholarship, the Dead Sea Scrolls. One of these discusses the breach with the temple, focusing on the calendar and the law, and could possibly be a letter from the Teacher of Righteousness to the Wicked Priest, that is, the leader of Qumran to Jonathan, the high priest and ruler. These new sources supplement what we already knew from the ancient literary sources, specifically Pliny the Elder, Philo of Alexandria, and Josephus.

Pliny the Elder wrote his encyclopedic *Natural History* in the first century CE. He asserts that the Essenes are "remarkable beyond all the other tribes in the whole world, as it has no women and has renounced all sexual desire, has no money, and has only palm trees for company." He found it fascinating that a celibate community could survive, even with the never-ending influx of refugees from life's tribulations. Pliny's description admittedly lacks detail and his focus on sex, or rather the lack of it, reflects a certain superficiality, but he provides one important detail: the sect's location. He places it in the desert on the west coast of the Dead Sea just north of Ein Gedi. In fact, this is the location of Qumran, exactly where the Dead Sea Scrolls were discovered, thus establishing that the scrolls were connected to the Essenes.

Philo was a hellenized Jew who lived in Alexandria from about 20 BCE to 50 CE. His goal was to combine the philosophical systems of Plato with Moses using allegory. Philo argued that the Hebrew scriptures were the source of truth and the basis of Greek philosophy. He held the Essenes in high regard as a concrete example of his philosophical views. They were not "word catchers," an allusion to the Pharisees, but rather lived their philosophy. They were devoted to the service of God and resolved to "preserve their minds in a state of holiness and purity." They renounced the material world, seeking instead moral wealth. To facilitate this, the Essenes left the cities, which were populated by the wicked, rejected their families, and set up their own communities. According to Philo, the goal of the Essenes was to remove themselves from temptation. They gave away all their personal property, including slaves, so as not to covet what others possessed. In order to suppress bodily passion, the Essenes renounced sex. Philo states that they did this "because a woman is a selfish creature and one addicted to jealousy." The suppression of sexual desire, aided by working from sunrise to sunset, provided a man with true liberty. Philo was writing for a hellenized audience, both Jew and gentile, so it's not surprising that he portrayed the Essenes almost as stoics, personifying the highest level of moral and ethical integrity in the traditions of Greek philosophy.

Out of the three ancient literary sources, Josephus provides the most detailed and entertaining account. He compares the Essenes to the Pythagoreans, a Greek school of philosophy, even though there was no real connection at all between the beliefs of the two groups. It was simply a superficial comparison of their ascetic lifestyles intended as a point of reference for his gentile audience. Thankfully, he provides some colorful and exotic detail. Since the Essenes committed themselves to celibacy, members were recruited from the outside world. They were required to give up all their earthly possessions when they entered the initiation period, and were provided with simple white garments and sandals—worn until they fell apart—a loincloth, and a spade. Only the loincloth was worn during the freezing ritual baths required for purification before each meal. The spade was provided to ensure modesty before God. When a member of the sect defecated, he dug a foot-deep hole, squatted over it with his cloak draped over shoulders, and filled it back in when he was done. The Essenes strove to follow God's laws more strictly than anyone else, and their observation of the Sabbath was particularly strict. Meals were prepared the day before. They avoided lifting utensils and even relieving themselves. Prayer preceded every meal and, since they didn't recognize the temple, unsacrificed meat was served. The Essenes were committed pacifists, promising to harm no one, and every word spoken was considered an oath. When not working in the fields or practicing their craft, they studied the sacred texts. The Essenes were also respected for their medical abilities and skill at prophesying.

The rules were strict. A new member swore his faithfulness to God, promised to treat everyone justly, and committed himself to obey the leaders of the sect. All his possessions belonged to the group. Although the initiate could give anything to his fellow Essenes, he needed to ask permission to be charitable to his own family. Breaking any of the rules had severe consequences, including expulsion, essentially a death sentence if he still followed the sect's dietary rules. Some Essenes lived outside the community in the general population and were allowed to marry, but they still strictly followed the law. Since sex was permitted for those outside only for procreation, it was prohibited with a pregnant wife. Just as men were required to wear loincloths in the ritual baths for modesty, women needed to be fully clothed.

Some scholars believe that the Essenes initially broke off from the Sadducees at the beginning of the Hasmonean period. Their strict interpretation of the written law and their rejection of the Pharisees' use of oral tradition support this viewpoint. However, their theology points to important differences with the Sadducees. Most importantly, the Essenes accepted the notion of an afterlife. Josephus gives this a philosophical twist:

> They teach the same doctrines as the sons of Greece. The body is
> corrupt and impermanent, but the soul is immortal. Good souls
> float to paradise and bad ones descend to Hades and are punished
> without end.

He maintains that they taught this doctrine not only because they believed in the afterlife but also because they wanted to encourage virtue. Furthermore, unlike the Sadducees who believed in free will, the Essenes took a position even more extreme than that of the Pharisees: a strict belief in predestination. Man was totally ruled by his fate.

Josephus hints at a mythical component of the views of the Essenes. However, this goes even deeper than he suggests. Their separation from the temple, the leaders of which they considered illegitimate, probably exacerbated this tendency as well. Our knowledge of the Essenes has been greatly increased by the discovery of the Dead Sea Scrolls. These documents represent a large collection of papyrus and parchment scrolls and scroll fragments that contain portions of the Hebrew Bible, apocryphal texts—including Aramaic fragments of the book of Enoch—from the Second Temple period, and documents from the sect itself. While some scholars believe they might have been hidden there immediately prior to the siege of Jerusalem during the great revolt, the consensus is that they were part of the Essenes' library. This view is reinforced by archeological evidence. The ruins include ritual baths and a large communal dining area. Animal bones were also found there, proving they ate meat.

One fragment, coded 4 QMMT, is very intriguing. Written around 150 BCE, it appears to be part of the letter written by the Teacher of Righteousness to the Wicked Priest. It lays out his objections to the way the temple was being run and advocates strictly following the law. It exhorts the Wicked Priest to understand these teachings and admonishes him to "strengthen your counsel and put you far from thoughts of evil." Another scroll, the "Manual of Discipline," rejects money and calls for a life of poverty. "The Damascus Covenant" argues against polygamy, which was still not prohibited by the law. On the other hand, the scrolls reflect the misogyny ingrained into their psyche. In a wisdom poem entitled "The Seductresses," the writer uses the metaphor of a harlot to warn against the attraction of false doctrines. One stanza reads:

> In the city square she veils herself,
> And she stands at the gates of towns
> She will never rest from whoring

The Dead Sea Scrolls also show that there was a strong mythical element in the beliefs of the sect, combining apocalyptic and eschatological beliefs with messianic undertones. There were dualistic qualities as well: the Children of the Elect versus the Children of Darkness; the Teacher of Righteousness versus the Wicked Priest. Finally, these sources strongly suggest that the resurrection that the Essenes envisioned was a physical one, not the Platonic transmigration of souls described by Philo and alluded to by Josephus.

It is intriguing how the Essenes relate to the other sects. Ironically, even though they rebelled against the leaders of the temple, their rigid views toward the law reflect those of the Sadducees and high priests and reject the use of oral law and tradition advocated by the Pharisees. On the other hand, both the Pharisees and Essenes were open to mythical interpretations of man's dilemma, and both believed in an afterlife. It's almost as if once the Essenes had separated themselves from the temple their imagination was set free and ran wild. Moreover, all three sects set boundaries, embracing their identity as Jews. The Sadducees were perhaps the least strict. In earlier times they were open to Hellenistic influences and at the time of Jesus they accepted Roman rule. The Pharisees created stronger barriers in their desire to obey the laws of the temple in everyday life. They did not remove themselves from society but set themselves apart as a morally positive influence. The Essenes built walls, not barriers. Like the monks of the Middle Ages, they removed themselves from their own families and communities to avoid temptation. It would be wrong, however, to view the sects too rigidly. Not only did they use the same language of temple and Torah, reflecting their deep commitment to Judaism, but they also came from the elites and sub-elites, the people who had the wealth and time to observe and interpret the law. They came from the rank-and-file priesthood, the temple staff, the scribes, and the families of rich merchants, officials, and landowners. They were not born into a sect but chose it voluntarily. Josephus even admits that not all Essenes chose celibacy and communal life. Some lived in the city and towns as members of the larger community. The world of the Jewish sects reflected the diversity and vibrancy of the society itself.

An understanding of the religious environment of the time of Jesus sheds important light on the Gospels. The law and the Torah were integral to Jewish life, and Jesus never rejected them. However, much like the Pharisees, Jesus was not afraid to reinterpret the law, but he did it in a way that ironically borrowed from the Sadducees. He was always looking for original intent in the Torah. As for the Essenes, taking a vow of poverty and rejecting one's family and community was not at all alien to Judaism at that time. A belief that poverty and separation could help someone find righteousness divided Jews from the rest of the ancient world. From this perspective, Jesus's expectations that his disciples sacrifice everything to follow him and his admonition to the rich young man to give up all his possessions do not sound quite so strange or radical. Nor were ideas of an afterlife, final judgment, apocalypse, or even the notion of a messiah

uncommon at the time. In effect, Jesus took the many strands of this profoundly rich intellectual and spiritual world and wove them together in a
profoundly revolutionary manner.

Chapter 6

Who Wrote the Gospels?

EVEN ACCEPTING THAT THE Gospels were inspired by the word of God, their creation is still a very complicated story. Who wrote them, when did they do it, and in what order were they written? Why were the Gospels written years after Paul's letters, which had already presented a fully formed theology? Why are there four of them, and why do they often contradict each other? Finally, how did the story of Jesus finally take written form a generation after his death and resurrection? Before answering these questions, let's state the obvious. The Gospels sprang from the world where Jesus lived, a product of their time and place. But does this mean that they were merely products of their social and cultural environment, reflecting the needs of society and not necessarily telling the story of the real Jesus? This is a disturbing thought and an existential question. To answer it, we need to turn to the role of biblical criticism in approaching the Gospels.

Biblical criticism is not a modern phenomenon. The final compilation of the Torah under Ezra's direction, with its interweaving of the various strands of authorship, was a critical process. The selection of which Gospels would form the official canon of the church required a critical evaluation of all the potential candidates while also confronting the contradictions between those that were finally accepted. The early church fathers, most notably Origen and St. Augustine, grappled with many of the same issues we do today, using allegory to solve some of the more obvious issues, such as internal contradiction, much like their successors in the Middle Ages and the Reformation.

Modern biblical criticism began with Thomas Hobbes and Baruch Spinoza in the seventeenth century. Hobbes argued that anything in the Bible that did not conform to natural law, such as miracles, had to be removed. Spinoza rejected miracles as well; they were simply visions or dreams. He also questioned the authorship of many of the books of the Bible. For instance, he was highly skeptical that Moses wrote the Torah, a view accepted now but revolutionary in the seventeenth century. Genre was also an important issue to Spinoza. The story of Adam and Eve was not history in his eyes but rather a parable. Perhaps Spinoza's most radical argument was the distinction between "meaning" and "truth" in the Bible. A biblical event might not be literally true but still have meaning. This was a key distinction and an important departure from using allegory as a cure-all. Bottom line: Spinoza analyzed the Bible like any other book, acknowledging its inconsistencies and contradictions while still accepting its core teachings concerning God and faith.

During the eighteenth-century enlightenment, biblical critics became even more skeptical, questioning the very foundation of belief. These thinkers included the Scottish philosopher David Hume, a confirmed atheist, and the English historian Edward Gibbon, who blamed Christianity for the fall of Rome and destruction of classical civilization. Others embraced Deism, the notion of God as the clockmaker of the universe with little control over our lives. In this type of environment, biblical criticism became more of a weapon against religion rather than a tool for leading us to a greater understanding of the Bible.

Biblical criticism as we know it today emerged in Protestant Germany during the late eighteenth century. Its practitioners were committed to a scientific critique of the sacred text while still accepting its relevance and truth. Johann Salomo Semler, a Lutheran theologian, believed that we can critically study the Bible without compromising its theological message. His successors in nineteenth century Germany continued to delve deeply into the Bible in a critical fashion while also searching for the "historical" Jesus. They established the order of the Gospels based on internal literary criticism, which included references or inferences to the destruction of the temple in 70 CE. It was established that Mark was written first, just before or right after that event, followed by Matthew and Luke in the late 70s or 80s, and finally John around 100 CE. Not only was the proper order of the Gospels confirmed, it also became apparent that the first three books were very different from the last, John. Mark, Matthew, and Luke are called the Synoptic Gospels because they follow a similar narrative or "synopsis" despite their differences and contradictions. Based on a common oral tradition, they tell many of the same stories in slightly different ways, using short, pithy sentences that explain what it took to enter the kingdom of heaven. John, on the other hand, presents a more theologically integrated and sophisticated work, composed of long, often eloquent, dialogues that focus on Jesus as the Son of God.

A dilemma, termed the "synoptic problem," emerged when it was determined that Mark, not Matthew, was the first Gospel. Although Matthew and Luke drew on Mark, they also contained other materials not in it. Where did these come from? It was hypothesized that another extinct source existed, a list of the sayings of Jesus written in either Aramaic or Greek that was called "Q," standing for the German word *quelle* for "source." This consensus became the catalyst for form criticism.

Form criticism sprang to life in Germany in the 1920s. It used the methods and even the trendy jargon of folklore studies. The form critics reconfigured Q as primarily an oral collection of the sayings and stories about Jesus. They believed these reminiscences were the sources of the Gospels. The problem in their eyes was the mutation of the story as it evolved, which could result in the story written in Gospels being very different from the actual historical event. In fact, it could have no relation to the real Jesus at all, making it simply a construct developed to mold the beliefs of the community in a way that met its needs. The form critic aimed to peel back the layers of the story to find the original narrative. Not an easy task since the oral tradition they imagined was fluid, opaque, and almost impossible to pin down.

Nevertheless, this approach was a valuable addition to the methodology of biblical criticism. It placed the creation of the Gospels smack in the middle of their social environment, maintaining that the narratives themselves were highly influenced by the communities in which they were written. If used correctly, they provide a vital perspective for interpreting the Gospels. However, like many academic theories, form criticism has its downside. It posited a problem that really didn't exist and developed a jargon that obscured its lack of success in achieving concrete results. Further, if this approach is taken to its logical extremes, the implications are profoundly nihilistic. If the Gospels are truly a product of their local community and don't really tell the story of Jesus, what value do they have beyond being mere historical artifacts? Moreover, a discipline based on folklore studies will ultimately diminish the Gospels, turning them into fairy tales with Jesus depicted merely as a folk hero.

Let's briefly summarize form criticism and parse some of the jargon. The "forms" are literary models transmitted orally before they were written down. Each one represented a particular form or method of narration. These include paradigms, or models for preachers, short stories followed by the sayings of Jesus, miracle stories, historical narratives, and legends. Myth, according to the form critics, underlined the cosmic significance of the charismatic cult hero. In the case of Jesus in the Synoptic Gospels, this would include his baptism, temptation, and transfiguration as well as the essential core of Christianity, the passion story and the resurrection, the oldest components of the tradition. Like folktales, each form reflected certain similarities in the way the story was related. For example, when Jesus performed a miracle, almost always it was recounted that the crowd was astonished. Ironically, a dissimilarity in a story increases the probability in form critics' eyes that it's genuine because it went against the traditional form. The smallest unit of the oral sources were called pericopes, Greek for "cut arounds," which were the individual sayings or stand-alone components of the narrative. The forms and the pericopes were orally transmitted by tradents, the storytellers. Finally, the form of the narrative was constantly modified by the *Sitz im Leben*, German for "place in life," which we would call the social and cultural context.

The terminology is pedantic. The term "form," for example, alludes to Plato. The original saying or story in Platonic terms would be the ideal or true one, with each following one a mere distorted reflection of the original. However, complaints about the jargon are minor when compared to the ultimate implications of form criticism. The stories themselves become fluid, or free-floating, oral transmissions changed during each telling or performance. The idea of finding the original form by breaking it down unit by unit, going back and peeling them off, might sound compelling but is virtually impossible to accomplish. In a sense the story becomes a function of the community's needs; the liturgy of the church in effect drove the narrative. One can't even be sure if the sayings were from Jesus. Finally, the Gospels are not aimed at a universal audience but rather are restricted to their individual communities.

In the second half of the twentieth century a new approach called redaction criticism developed, not to replace form criticism but to refine it. This technique was very productive in explaining the development of the Old Testament, and make a certain amount of sense in approaching the Gospels. It perceived the Gospels not as oral traditions haphazardly stitched together but as reshaped and rewritten by redactors. However, the pivotal problem remains. Are the Gospels firmly grounded on Jesus and his teachings or merely a product of the social and cultural environment of the redactors who collated them? The redaction critics moved beyond the oral confines of form criticism but still viewed the Gospels as products of the communities for whom they were written. Consequently, Jesus still remains distant and detached from the text.

Let's get on firmer ground by approaching this problem from a different perspective. If Jesus lived today, how would his good news be transmitted? He would go viral. People would video him with their cell phones, put it on Instagram, and tweet about him incessantly. Jesus would be on LinkedIn and have a Facebook page. In other words, it would be all about social media. It was very much the same two thousand years ago. Think of it this way: Oral transmission was the social media of the ancient world, and it was nowhere near as primitive as we might think. The place to start, therefore, is a discussion of literacy, or the lack of it, in the ancient world and the role of oral communication. Only by understanding the literary and the oral traditions in the world of Jesus, with their intimate interconnections, can we gain insight into how the Gospels were written.

For centuries classical scholars assumed that a society that possessed such sophisticated literature as the ancients had to be highly literate. Why would Virgil, Plato, Thucydides, or Ovid write if they didn't have a large audience? Would great works of literature, poetry, philosophy, and history be produced for an illiterate population? The classical historian William V. Harris exploded the myth of a high ancient literacy rate in a seminal monograph published in 1989. His conclusion was startling: About 10 percent of the population was literate. Moreover, the definition of literacy that he employed was broad. You were literate if you could read or write a simple statement concerning your daily life. In effect, the ancient world had high literary standards, but it was inhabited by illiterates. The development of literacy is a complicated story, and the sources are patchy. Harris's conclusions are based on intelligent inference rather than quantitative research, which the paucity of hard evidence makes impossible. However, after an initial pushback, most classical scholars, although they might quibble about the details, agree that the rate of literacy in the ancient world was much lower than previously accepted.

As revolutionary as the development of literacy in ancient times might have been, by our standards it was limited, an intermediate stage between orality and literacy. One scholar, Keith Hopkins, makes a provocative point that underlines the revolutionary aspect of literacy. Money and literacy have a shared characteristic: they transcend space and time. In each case you need not be face-to-face with your counterpart; money is to the economy what literacy is to the world of ideas. Paul's letters are an example of this. He's able to communicate with churches across the Mediterranean world. But if Paul were living near a particular church, he would not have bothered to write; oral communication would have been preferable. Oral communication was still highly valued, sometimes carrying even more prestige than writing. The Pharisees believed the oral law augmented the written law. If you could deal with someone face-to-face, you did just that. Even legal agreements could be oral. To many people, the written word was suspicious, almost magical, a medium that spread deceit.

People's memories in ancient times were more highly developed than ours. Mnemonic devices were utilized to memorize even whole texts. One Roman consul during the republic was reputed to have known the names of every citizen. Education was based on memory. For example, literature was taught by students chanting the texts. Recitation and dictation were the twin pillars of pedagogy. Singing was as much a memorizing technique as it was an aesthetic exercise. In fact, when people read to themselves, they spoke the words out loud in a singsong manner. Caesar once commented when he heard someone in another room singing that he was either a poor singer or a very good reader. When an author published his work, it was often in the form of a recitation before an audience. If the emperor Augustus couldn't sleep, he didn't curl up with a mystery novel. He summoned a reader or storyteller.

Nevertheless, all this should not detract from the importance of literacy and its impact on civilization. It was essential for running the political bureaucracy. The Roman army required literate centurions to run the legions. It was also essential for commerce, especially over long distances. Literature could be preserved and shared with a wider audience. Aside from the mistrust of a mostly illiterate population, there was another side of the coin. Sacred texts like the Torah and later the New Testament gained a mystical, almost magical, power. The written word was a sign of the divine. The text did not merely represent but was in a real sense the very word of God. The fact that riots ensued in Jerusalem when a Roman soldier desecrated the Torah reinforces this point. The act was not viewed as symbolic; the physical object itself had enormous prestige because of the sacred nature of the actual Hebrew letters on the pages. The high status accorded to scribes was derived from their ability to inscribe these letters on the sacred scrolls. We can witness this reverence for the written word today when the Torah is removed from the ark in a modern synagogue.

However, mass literacy was never achieved and there was not even a demand for it. Yes, as Harris points out, "If fortune set the individual among the literate, that was a golden gift," but it did not follow that citizens were expected to read. Nor was a high level of literacy considered necessary for the elite. Slaves could read and write for them. Literacy was controlled by the elite but not always performed by its members. Neither was there a large market demand for books or an incentive to mass produce them. Usually, they were loaned to friends or simply copied. Cost was a major factor. One sheet of papyrus would cost around forty dollars in modern currency. The idea that there were large publishing houses mass producing manuscripts copied by slaves is simply a myth.

Let's dig deeper and deal specifically with literacy in Palestine at the time the Gospels were written. It reflected the situation in the larger empire but had its own unique characteristics. There was more than one language. Greek, not Latin, was the language of provincial and urban administration and commerce. It was the chosen method of communication by the hellenized elites. Koine, or Alexandrian Greek, was the dialect of the eastern Mediterranean. Aramaic, on the other hand, was used in the countryside and on the streets. It had been the administrative language of the Persian Empire, which ruled Judea for over two hundred years and a written form of it took root at that time. The rise of vernacular Aramaic was complicated, but for centuries the Jews of Palestine had been interacting with neighboring peoples in it and gradually adopted it themselves. Hebrew, however, was the language of the sacred scriptures and the vernacular of many Jews. Written, or classical Hebrew, was difficult, its pronunciation differing from the vernacular, and the grammar and vocabulary complex and archaic. The literary language contained up to twenty-five consonants, the vernacular only seventeen. It took many years of education for a person to read Hebrew publicly. Greek with its more simplified script was easier for most literate people to read and write than Hebrew. This helps explain why the Gospels were written in Greek and not Hebrew. Yet we should not underestimate the importance of Hebrew. Fergus Millar, the renowned Oxford classical historian, once wrote that the Jews, singular among the peoples of the Roman Empire, not only possessed a long-recorded history, but it also was constantly reinterpreted and acted upon. This history was recorded in the Old Testament in Hebrew, and these texts were in a real sense the soul of the nation. They defined the national identity in a way that allowed the Jews to envision the creation of their own independent state. The elevated importance of a written Hebrew sacred text also underlined the need for written Gospels for the new religion of Christianity. Oral narratives would not suffice.

If literacy across the ancient world was correlated to power, the ability to read Hebrew scripture was essential in order to establish one's place at the pinnacle of the Jewish social hierarchy, which was based not on wealth but rather on religious prestige. This educated elite included the priests and scribes whose job was to interpret scripture, but also the Pharisees who challenged their monopoly. Since the sacred texts controlled religious ideology, access to them was critical. Another group recognized this reality. These were the elite landowners, often overlapping with the Pharisees. They could afford the scrolls and the time and education to learn to read them. They read them to their families, neighbors, and in public at the synagogue. This provided not only personal satisfaction but also the status and prestige that mere wealth could never attain.

But what did it mean to read a book at that time? First, reading was intensive, not extensive. The Roman philosopher Seneca once observed that reading too many books was a distraction; it's best to focus on the tried-and-true ones. Books were read repeatedly. It was difficult to find new titles. There were less than one thousand texts in Palestine written at that time in Hebrew and Aramaic. Books were read out loud in a singsong fashion while reading to an audience or even to oneself. Reading, orality, and memorization were intimately intertwined. Literary texts had mnemonic qualities that allowed the reader to memorize it. There is a story of a rabbi who didn't have a scroll of the book of Esther available to him during Purim. He knew it by heart, but rather than simply reciting it, he wrote it out by hand and then read it. This highlights not only the strength of orality and the role of memory but also the mystical power of the written word, the very scratches on the scroll being seen as the real word of God. The degree of reverence for the written text was unique to the ancient world, very different from today.

Palestine was a multilingual society with Aramaic, not Hebrew, the dominant spoken language. However, conversation often shifted from one language to another and each borrowed words from the others. There are numerous examples of this in the Gospels and Acts. When Paul was being attacked by an angry mob in Jerusalem, Roman soldiers intervened. When the apostle appealed to their leader, the first thing the tribune replied was, "Do you speak Greek?" Arguably Jesus was fluent in Greek as well as Aramaic and Hebrew. However, the multiplicity of languages could also inhibit communication, even among Jews. The miracle related to this problem in Acts during Pentecost reflects this. The Holy Spirit made it possible for the apostles to be understood by all the pilgrims from across the Roman Empire, and beyond, visiting Jerusalem.

What do we know about the actual level of literacy in Palestine around the time of Jesus? Luckily there's a source that provides provocative clues about this question that has been mined by Michael Owen Wise, an expert in Semitic languages. These sources were discovered in 1953 near Ein Gedi, a Jewish village in the Judean desert just west of the Dead Sea. They're called the Bar Kokhba texts because they were hidden in caves there during the second great Jewish revolt led by Simon Bar Kokhba in the early 130s CE. They are a treasure trove of mostly legal documents with a smaller number of letters, including the archives of the very same Babatha, whose legal and marital issues were discussed in chapter 5. Wise has brilliantly exploited them to explore the topic of ancient literacy in a unique way. Aramaic, Hebrew, and Greek represent the language of most of the documents, but they also contain some writings in Nabatean along with a few bits of Latin and Arabic. The names of about four hundred people can be found in them. The content of the contracts and other legal documents indicate that they come from the wealthy top quarter of society. Wise uses these texts and especially the signatures of the signatories and witnesses to estimate the level of literacy and gain insights on the degree of each language's proliferation.

Before turning to the actual levels of literacy that this source implies, we need to examine some of the broader insights it provides into the interplay of the languages native to the region. The documents reinforce that Aramaic was by far the most popular language. Most of the signatures were in it as well as the letters and legal documents. However, the texts were composed in the vernacular, not literary, Aramaic. The vernacular included loan words from both Hebrew and Greek. The use of the common spoken language for writing points to the distinction between scholarly literacy and functional literacy. It also points to another interesting fact. While almost all Jews spoke Aramaic in their daily life, they were not able to understand books written in it. Conversely, despite its relative difficulty and its differences from the vernacular, when peopled did learn to read Hebrew it would be in the classical version. Obviously, the ability to read sacred texts and the prestige that this brought in the community was a major factor, but it was also, considering the challenge of Hellenism during the last couple of centuries, a statement of cultural and even national identity. Written Greek, to a lesser extent, was preferred to literary Aramaic. It was the language of government administration and business. A man on the make would find it very useful. Besides that, just as Aramaic was the language of the winners under Persian rule, Greek had had that characteristic since the conquests of Alexander. And as we have seen, if you could speak Greek, it was easier to learn to read than Hebrew because of its closer connection to the vernacular. About one third of the village leaders could speak Greek and half of those could read it well enough to understand a book.

When assessing the actual levels of literacy, a few factors must be kept in mind. The letters and documents found at Ein Gedi are representative of the elite, who Wise estimates made up about 20 percent of the total population. The literacy levels for the general population can only be inferred from this, and the evidence also suggests that women were largely illiterate. About two thirds of the signatories and witnesses were literate and half of them were most likely literary literates, that is, they could read a book. That would amount to about 40 percent of the adult male elite. As far as the general adult male population is concerned, the numbers were obviously much lower. About 15 percent could make a signature and between 5 and 10 percent were literary literates. As far as the numbers for the total population are concerned, it was even lower, in the low single digits. As Wise put it: "Only one in forty people could crack a book." However, not being able to crack a book would not inhibit anyone from listening to the Gospels being read out loud.

Just as revolutionary as the written Gospels was the physical appearance of the texts. Traditionally ancient literature was written on papyrus scrolls. This included not only the works of the great Roman and Greek authors but also the books of the Old Testament. However, the Gospels were written in codex form. The word codex comes from the Latin *caudex*, which means block of wood. This refers to the pieces of wood that were attached together with strings or leather thongs to make an ancient notebook. At first, each of the two boards had wax on the inside. This allowed the writer to take notes with a stylus and then erase them, making these notebooks indispensable for students and useful for business and finance. Poets and other authors could also use the codex for first drafts, which could later be copied on a scroll. As many as ten tablets could be bound together and stored in archives. However, other materials could be inserted instead of wax, including thin sheets of wood veneer, and these could also be used for notes as well as letters, drafts, and documents along with financial and military records. By the end of the first century CE, Romans were beginning to insert parchment and even papyrus between the covers. By the time of the late empire, the codex began to replace scrolls, becoming the forerunner of the modern book. However, the codex, not the scroll, was the preferred method of recording the books of the New Testament right from the start. Why did the early Christians choose recording their sacred texts in this lowly notebook form rather than using scrolls, the preferred format for serious literature and sacred texts?

The answer is not totally clear, but some of the possibilities cast light on the transmission of belief in early Christianity. If the Gospels had been written in Hebrew, the language of God, they would have been inscribed on scrolls. It would have been an abomination to do otherwise. However, both the Epistles and Gospels were written in common Greek, making the more prestigious format less imperative. The letter format of the Epistles also worked well in a codex. There were other practical reasons. A codex was convenient and easily portable. A single Gospel would fill one scroll, but all four could fit into one codex. Codices were also easier to study and check references. A less formal approach influenced the content as well. The Latin and Greek written on scrolls were in effect a "river of words," with no spaces between them and no division into paragraphs. Imagine trying to analyze and a study a text in such a format. In codices, there were marks separating paragraphs and abbreviations for frequently repeated words, especially those representing the divine.

Elite literature in the ancient world was perceived as a final, polished, artistic product. Anything that didn't conform to this ideal was considered, often unjustly, as second rate, unfinished and unworthy of expensive scrolls. This not only included lecture notes, letters, and commentaries, but also works that we would now consider of a very high level. Even Caesar's books on the Gallic and civil wars were considered unfinished despite their succinct eloquence, because they were swiftly composed in a simple, straightforward style. One cannot deny that the Gospels, as profound and vivid as they are, reflect some of these characteristics. It was a tradition of the early church that Mark recorded the oral preaching of Peter in Rome, which was in effect taking notes. The Gospels were a part of the genre of ancient biography, but the mixing together of biographical narrative and religious teaching also provided the characteristics of more informal commentaries.

Social class also played a part in the adaptation of the codex. There are many representations of codices and scrolls in the iconography of Roman art. Students, clerks, and even tax collectors are shown with codices, while senior officials and heads of households are depicted holding scrolls. This is a not-so-subtle reminder that scrolls were the province of the elites while codices belonged with those who were socially inferior. Early Christians were not normally recruited among the elites. If literate, they would have been more comfortable handling a codex than a scroll. Practicality and accessibility trumped snob appeal.

Since there was no clear demarcation between literary and oral communication in Jesus's world, writing was not meant solely for the larger audience and talking for small ones. The information network of that time was complex and multidimensional, intersecting and overlapping on many levels. Believers traveled from place to place, preaching the "good news." The Gospels were read, or performed, in front of congregations consisting mostly of illiterate people. And if the form critics have taught us anything, it's that original sources for the Gospels were overwhelmingly oral. A written text was indispensable for the growth of the faith, but the level of its dependability is subject to the authenticity of its oral sources. If the form critics are right, oral sources are unreliable. They reflect the needs of the community rather than recording the actual words of Jesus. However, is it possible that they accurately recount his life and work? To answer this, we need to shift focus and explore the other side of the equation, trying to understand what the oral tradition entailed in first century Palestine.

The study of oral traditions is an immense, interdisciplinary field involving folklore studies, comparative literature, and classics. Biblical criticism reflects only one aspect of it. As good a place as any to jump into the subject is by considering the work of a brilliant and eccentric Harvard scholar named Milman Parry. He was a classicist on the cusp of taking his field by storm; one scholar called him "the Darwin of Homeric studies." In order to develop his theory that the *Iliad* and *Odyssey* were at their core based on oral tradition and performance, Parry did field work during the 1930s in Bosnia, Serbia, and Croatia, observing and recording traditional storytellers. He wore traditional garb like his hero Lawrence of Arabia and packed a pistol as protection against the outlaws who infested the countryside of the former Yugoslavia. Unfortunately, he continued carrying his revolver when he arrived back in the States, packing it in his suitcase on a trip to Los Angeles in 1935. The gun either accidentally went off, killing the thirty-three-year-old instantly, or he was murdered by his wife, suicide being the least probable cause. The combination of a tragic young death and a flamboyant and romantic lifestyle only increased his reputation and added to his Indiana Jones like celebrity. Nevertheless, he was a truly remarkable scholar. His student Albert Lord continued his work, publishing the classic *The Singer of Tales* in 1960.

Why is Parry important to us? For a few reasons. The young American received his doctorate at the Sorbonne in the 1920s, exactly the time that form criticism was developing in Germany, and he also utilized the tools of folklore studies in approaching his subject. He shook up his field just like the form critics did theirs. He argued that the *Iliad* and *Odyssey* were the product of oral compositions, that is, performances, which were constantly altered by the epic storyteller in response to his audience. They were not reciting a written text but composing the epics as they went along. This approach diminished the creativity of Homer in the eyes of more traditional classicists, very much like the form critics put into question the very veracity of the Gospels. Moreover, Parry and Lord used similar terminology. They based their study on the analysis of forms or formulas, the recurring structures within the poems that moved the storyteller along or, as Lord described them, "chunks of language" inherited by the singer poets. Within that framework, each performance was different from those of its predecessors. Real creativity was displayed during the performance itself. This resulted in a fluidity and flexibility in the evolution of this oral tradition, much like the phenomenon imagined in the development of the Gospels by the form critics.

In short, form criticism was not unique but reflected theories of folklore that were in the intellectual air. However, Parry's approach has stood the test of time much better than that of the form critics. There is an important reason for this. The Homeric poems were performed for centuries before they were finally written down into anything approaching an authoritative edition. Therefore, their oral evolution in the way Parry and Lord describe makes intuitive sense. On the other hand, the time from the crucifixion of Jesus to the writing of the Gospels was very short. The form critics were in effect trying to put a square peg into a round hole, using a method meant for a much longer time span, at least half a millennium, for a mere generation. Also, the nature of the two oral traditions, epic poetry and the oral sources for the Gospels, were different, representing entirely separate genres. Parry and Lord believed that oral composition was not merely a prelude to its literary presentation but that it was as equal in literary quality as its written progeny. The oral sources for the Gospels, however, were a very different animal. Rather than being a literary creation, they were mere collections of episodic events and sayings. The sad truth is that the form critics, bedazzled by the folklorists of the time, chose an inappropriate model to study the relationship of oral tradition to the Gospels.

Kenneth E. Bailey, a scholar and Presbyterian minister, provides another perspective. Born in 1930 to missionary parents, he grew up in Egypt, Sudan, and Ethiopia, and after his ordination spent the bulk of his career in the Middle East. Building on his fluency in Arabic and his village pastoral work, Bailey wrote several influential books, which viewed the New Testament through "Middle Eastern eyes." This approach was particularly productive in his exegesis, or critical examination and interpretation, of the parables. However, what's relevant to us is an article he wrote in an obscure journal, *Asia Journal of Theology*, in 1991. It became an important building block for a group of biblical scholars who were in the process of dismantling form criticism.

Like Parry, Bailey did research in the field. He was in effect a biblical anthropologist. He became intimately involved with Middle Eastern village life and closely observed how oral traditions were transmitted. Bailey not only observed the evening storytelling sessions but also participated in them himself. He categorized the oral tradition that he observed into three broad models. The first of these he called "informal uncontrolled" tradition. This was precisely the type of transmission that the form critics envisioned: constantly evolving, "fluid, and plastic." Bailey admitted this model did exist in the modern Middle East, but it was used for spreading rumor and gossip. On the other extreme was what he called "formal controlled" tradition. This involves complete memorization. It exists in the form of word for word recitation of the Qu'ran. In fact, the first major reaction against form criticism, emanating from Scandinavia in the 1960s, embodied this mode of oral tradition. Burger Gerhaedsson studied the early rabbinic tradition and applied it to the early Christians. Disciples of the rabbis were expected to memorize the teaching of their masters in their exact words. He conjectured that the followers of Jesus did the same by memorizing his teaching word for word. However, this appears too rigid, relying on the assumption that the disciples would have mimicked a tradition that developed a century or more later. But between the two extremes, the totally uncontrolled and totally controlled, existed a middle way.

Bailey called this the "informal controlled" tradition, which he observed during the actual storytelling sessions. The stories were not memorized, but the participants and listeners made certain the integrity of the narrative was preserved. There was not a single storyteller. Elders and socially prominent men of the village told the stories or recited the poems. The degree of flexibility allowed depended on the genre. If proverbs or poems were being recited, a missed word would elicit a correction from the audience. More latitude was given for recounting community history or sharing parables. It was a performance; the storyteller could alter the story, but the punch line or conclusion needed to be accurate. This is analogous to the oral transmission of the *Iliad*. The singer of the song could change the dramatic details in his performance—the parries and thrusts of combat, for example—but Achilles always defeats Hector. The same was true in the village renditions witnessed by Bailey. There was a constant interaction between the person telling his story and the audience that provided both flexibility and control. This suggests that the authenticity of the Gospels could have been maintained even if small details were changed. The oral rendition would have remained lively and engaging, but informal control ensured that the story would not shift to meet the whims or needs of a particular moment.

This paradigm makes much more intuitive sense than form criticism, but an important question remains. Who exactly were the people who told the story of Jesus and controlled the narrative? This is where it gets very interesting, going well beyond Bailey's research. Yes, the oral narrative was probably controlled like he described, but it was not overseen by unnamed village elders, but rather by named eyewitnesses who had observed the events. In short, the very people who knew Jesus. This is a profound insight with far reaching implications that raise two other important questions. First, if the Gospels were not oral narratives evolving from specific community needs, what literary genre were they? Second, were the Gospels aimed solely at the community in which they were written or were they meant for a wider audience? Before answering these questions, however, we need to identify who these "eyewitnesses" were and what was their relation to the Gospels.

Biblical scholars are becoming increasingly receptive to the notion that the Gospels are based on eyewitness testimony, but the scholar most identified with this thesis is Richard Bauckham. He was trained as a historian at Cambridge University and later turned to biblical scholarship. Training as a historian was critical to his intellectual development. Rather than adopting a theoretical model and molding the facts to fit it, he studied the sources, in this case the Gospels themselves and the writings of the early church fathers. The conclusion he came to is deceptively simple but profoundly important. The Gospels were based on eyewitness testimony provided by witnesses named within them. The core of these named persons includes but are not limited to the twelve disciples themselves. Not only did these eyewitnesses orally transmit the story of Jesus, but they also controlled the narrative, making sure it wasn't changed. They weren't simply relating single events or individual sayings, but rather controlling the entire narrative.

Bauckham employs internal evidence to buttress his argument. For example, Peter's prominence both in the beginning of Mark and at the end, where his inclusion was not necessary for the sake of the narrative, strongly suggests he was the key eyewitness. This way of specifying the witness, called "inclusio" by literary critics, is not limited to the Gospels. It is a common literary technique utilized for analyzing ancient histories and biographies, where personal testimony was considered the most valuable source. That Peter was the chief source for Mark is extremely important because Mark in turn was the most important source for Matthew and Luke. It is also likely that Peter related his account to John Mark, a disciple mentioned in Acts and the Epistles. The Gospel of John also made use of Mark, but Bauckham believes that the primary witness there was the writer himself, John, the "beloved disciple."

It is not only internal evidence that supports this thesis. The primary importance of eyewitness testimony was a key component of the whole genre of ancient biography. Indeed, right at the beginning of Luke, the author writes in his dedication, another characteristic of the genre, that his account was handed down to him by "those who from the beginning were eyewitnesses and servants of the word." Could it be clearer? Eyewitnesses were also the source for the apostle Paul, who related in Galatians that he spent two weeks in Jerusalem with Peter. As one scholar has wryly noted, they didn't spend the time talking about the weather.

This focus on the value of oral, eyewitness testimony is further reinforced in the writing of Papias, the bishop of Hierapolis, a city in what is now modern-day Turkey. He wrote a long theological work in the beginning of the second century. Unfortunately, it has been lost but sections of it are quoted in the works of other early church fathers. Hierapolis was located at the crossroads of two major Roman highways, one running east to west from Antioch to Ephesus and the other northwest to Smyrna. All three of these were major cities of the Roman East and important centers of the early Christian movement. As a young man, around 80 CE, Papias interviewed many respected teaching elders, who had learned from the direct eyewitnesses of Jesus, as they passed through Hierapolis. It was the great roads of the Roman Empire that provided Papias with the social network needed to undertake his research. In the prologue of the treatise that he wrote years later, Papias stressed two important points. First, he wasn't just interviewing anyone. They had to be eyewitnesses or closely connected to them. Remember, they were only a generation removed from the events in the Gospels. Most of the original disciples had already died, but a couple, including John the Elder, still lived. Second, he stressed that the most reliable information came from "a living and surviving voice." He was not talking about mere hearsay but rather solid information from a credible source. It was an ancient example of a policeman or journalist today demanding "just the facts, please."

Papias explicitly asserted that Peter was the source of Mark. He stated that an elder had told him that Mark had recorded everything that Peter told him about Jesus. This source explained that Peter's testimony had not been related in a final narrative form, but rather that he presented it by sharing *chreiai*, or "anecdotes," about Jesus. This implies that Mark arranged Peter's recollections into a linear narrative. This is crucially important. Papias was interviewing people in the early 80s, and the Gospel of Mark was written only a few years before. This did not reflect a story molded by amorphous oral transmission. It is testimony firmly based on close observation.

If the Gospels had been based on an ethereal and fluid oral tradition, changing and adjusting to communal needs as the form critics would have us believe, the text itself would not reflect reality but would rather have the characteristics of fiction or folklore. On the other hand, if it could be proved that the Gospels had a concrete connection to the real world around them, this would buttress our confidence that they embodied eyewitness testimony.

Bauckham does just that. He cites an Israeli historian by the name of Tal Ilan who recently published a list of all the recorded Jewish names in Palestine between 330 BCE and 200 CE. Ilan used literary sources to collate it, including Josephus, the New Testament, the Dead Sea Scrolls, and rabbinic texts, along with inscriptions and names on ossuaries or burial urns. This was in effect, as Bauckham observes, the equivalent of an ancient phone book. This allows for the calculation of the relative popularity of Jewish names. Simon and Joseph, for example, were the most popular male names while Mary and Salome were the female favorites. Bauckham focused on male names since they formed a much larger statistical sample. What he found was fascinating. The relative popularity of male names in the Gospels is closely correlated to those of the entire sample of the population. Why is this important? If the Gospels were not based on reliable testimony, were in fact derived from increasingly fictional communal oral transmissions, the odds of this direct correlation would be negligible. Let's put this in modern context. If the names found in a sample of newspapers in the United States mirrored those in the total population, we would not expect the same outcome from using a novel with its fictional characters formed from the author's imagination. Bauckham's analysis reinforces the belief that the Gospels are closely connected to and grounded on the world in which they were written.

If this is the case, who was the intended audience and what literary genre do the Gospels reflect? Let's deal with genre first. Once we understand the kind of literature the Gospels represent, it's much easier to define the audience. The growing consensus in biblical scholarship is that the Gospels are an example of the ancient genre of lives, *bioi* in Greek. This is not to be confused with a modern biography, which not only chronologically recounts its subject's life but also focuses on his or her personality, social relationships, and psychology, often over many hundreds of pages. Greek and Roman lives were much shorter and usually filled a single papyrus scroll. Although they recorded the subject's background and birth and the circumstances of his death, they did not provide a complete chronological biography. The narrative related anecdotes, speeches, and major events and focused on the subject's public life. The biographer's goal was not to provide an objective account based on historical evidence. Rather it was to defend or attack the subject and frequently conveys moral judgment.

Often disproportionate space was given to the subject's death, perhaps 10 to 20 percent of the text. The Gospels reflect all these characteristics, having much in common, for example, with Plutarch's Lives and Suetonius's Lives of the Twelve Caesars. They record Jesus's birth and background, provide anecdotes on his miracles and sayings, record sermons, and spend a relatively large amount of time on his death. The biblical scholar Richard Burridge has analyzed the texts of ancient biographies and found that a quarter to a third of the verbs relate to one person, the subject. The Gospels also reflect this characteristic, meaning that the Gospels are about one thing and one thing only: Jesus Christ. Other characters are secondary. Jesus's criticisms of his disciples for instance are not meant to tell us about them but rather to increase our understanding of him. Expounding an explicit theology is not the Gospels' goal. It is implicit, not explicit, explaining perhaps why the theology was first formulated in the Epistles. Also, ancient historians and biographers, much like journalists today, believed that eyewitness testimony was critical. Indeed, personal testimony, especially from those closely involved in the events, was considered superior to written sources. If we accept the fact that the Gospels are a part of this genre, and the arguments for this are extremely robust, the conclusion is straightforward: They should not be read, as the form and redaction critics would have us do, to understand more about the communities they were written for, but rather to learn about Jesus himself. Moreover, the structure of the Gospels, reflecting a specific genre, strongly suggest that they are not the output of some communal committee. Each one was written by one author.

The recognition that the Gospels are in the genre of ancient biography has important implications. If they were not solely the product of a specific church or community, they must have been aimed at a wider audience. Or to put it another way: Even if a Gospel was composed in a specific community, it does not follow that its message was restricted to it. This was also the case in Greek and Roman biography. The Roman historian Tacitus lived at the same time the Gospels were written. Besides his more famous histories, he wrote a biography defending his father-in-law Agricola, who served as governor of Britain under the immensely unpopular emperor Domitian. This work was not aimed only at his subject's family and friends but rather to defend his reputation to a much wider audience. On a much more profound level, the Gospels served a similar function. They were telling the story of Jesus not only to augment his reputation but more importantly to inspire and change people. This audience might include Christians suffering persecution, providing strength by the example of Jesus, but the Gospels were also written to attract converts. There are numerous instances where gentiles are portrayed in a positive manner, again implying a wider audience not limited to one specific group. Richard Burridge writes that the Gospels were "written by people for people about people." The people they were intended for stretched across the entire Mediterranean world.

The belief that the audience of the Gospels was restricted to the specific community is based on a distorted notion of social networking in the Roman world. People were moving around all the time by land and sea. There were Jews scattered throughout the empire who frequently visited the temple in Jerusalem on the high holy days. Paul and his followers traveled back and forth across the Mediterranean. Papias interviewed Christian leaders and teachers moving from place to place. Communication between churches was encouraged. Letters were sent between them. In a world lacking a modern postal system, messengers who were believers carried them.

What existed in effect was what one scholar, Michael Thompson, calls a "holy internet." This is a powerful metaphor. The Roman roads and sea lanes, protected by the Pax Romana, provided an "information superhighway." There were rest stops on the roads and milestones marking the way. The Egnatian Way stretched across the Balkans from Byzantium, modern Istanbul, to Dyrrachium on the Adriatic coast. It was easy to travel on it even during the winter. A traveler from Palestine or Syria could connect to it by crossing Asia Minor with its sophisticated road network connecting the rich cities of the region. After a brief voyage across the Adriatic, he could connect with the Appian Way and quickly head on to Rome. A person walking could cover fifteen to twenty-five miles a day and a courier on horse made about fifty. There were many travelers: merchants, government officials, teachers, students, pilgrims, artisans, actors, and even runaway slaves. The sea lanes were much faster but dangerous during the winter months. It was often the case that travelers would go by sea in one direction and by land in the other. The network servers of the holy internet were the churches where the traditions were collected, developed and transmitted. In the early Christian period, Jerusalem was the prime information hub, but there were other critical ones, including Rome, Antioch, Philippi on the Egnatian Way, Corinth, and Ephesus. The portal to faith was baptism. The protocol software was the hospitality provided by believers in the hubs. Hospitality served not only a practical role but also a spiritual one, spreading the word and bonding believers with each other. Early Christians hungered for news and had a strong desire to share their beliefs with fellow believers and potential converts. News traveled by letter, but the messenger provided an oral performance that was often just as important as the written text.

This notion of a holy internet is vitally important. It conforms to what we know about the society of the Roman world. It reflects the dynamic nature of both the world that Jesus lived in and the one in which early Christianity grew. It was neither static nor inward looking. The belief that somehow the Gospels were meant for a specific, isolated region, reflecting solely its need and concerns, runs totally against the grain of the evidence. The very nature of the Gospels, their genre and function, argue that they were meant to be shared. If the local community was meant to be the only audience, oral transmission would have sufficed. The theology was there; Paul ensured that. By writing it all down with Jesus as the central character, the authors of the Gospels not only defined and elaborated the faith, but they also provided a means to spread it. The fact that they still resonate with people today only confirms this universal quality.

Conclusion

THE DIRECTION OF BIBLICAL criticism over the last century had negative implications. Form criticism turned Jesus into a folk hero and a hazy one at that. The writers of the Gospels became merely "stenographers at the end of the tunnel," recording the words of wisdom of a teacher who lived a generation before. Redaction criticism marginally improved the situation. Nevertheless, the results were still far from satisfactory. The Gospels were simply a reflection of the community and did not really teach us about Jesus. The aim was to parse the Gospels to learn about these groups of early Christians. The *Sitz im Leben* of the form critics gradually became the object of the analysis, not Jesus himself. And rather than actually teaching us about the ancient Christian communities themselves, the reflections perceived in the mirror of history instead coincided with the opinions of the contemporary eyes looking into it, not reflecting historical truth but contemporary critical bias. Jesus was further away than ever before.

How could such an approach have dominated the curriculum of prestigious seminaries for such a long time? Why did serious scholars, mostly all of them believers, accept such jargon-infested speculation? Perhaps it was because they couldn't accept a literal interpretation of the Bible. Just too many weird things were going on in the text that were often contradictory as well. Modern biblical scholarship provided a cloak of respectability, a way to separate themselves from fundamentalist evangelicals. If Jesus disappeared from the story, it was a necessary sacrifice. The seminaries, like other prestigious academic institutions, were also infected by another academic malaise: post-modernism. This is the belief that there is no such thing as fact and truth. Everything is relative and every narrative has an equal claim to truth. In its own perverse way this has the same result as form criticism: The authentic Jesus melts away, adopting whatever persona the scholar provides him.

This is why the revolt against form criticism is so important. It takes Jesus from the realm of fairy tale and makes him real again. By accepting that the Gospels represent the well-developed genre of ancient biography, based on genuine eyewitness testimony, Christ becomes their living core. He is immediate, standing before the reader, not a phantom fabricated in an ever-changing oral tradition. Instead, the eyewitnesses spread the story in a well-greased social network. The written Gospels that emerged were aimed at a universal audience. Even their format, the practical, everyday codex, increased their impact.

Making Jesus real again, and placing him firmly in the world where he lived, makes understanding the historical context even more important. Looking at the Gospels as an historian not only provides a framework but also enhances our interpretation of them. This doesn't mean searching for the historical Jesus. That always ends badly; authors tend to fashion him to suit their own preconceptions. Nor does understanding the history contradict our primary motivation for reading the Bible: spiritual enrichment. What it does is provide a perspective for interpreting the meaning of the Scriptures. Knowing about the role of women in ancient Palestine, for example, can prevent us from imposing our own attitudes about gender, sexuality, abortion, and divorce on the subject, which only distorts our discernment of the text. This lack of historical context has motivated traditionalists to still believe that Mary Magdalene was a prostitute and some feminists to argue that she was the wife of Jesus. There is no evidence for either of these views beyond the ideology of their proponents.

Such an approach can lead to dangerous places. Morton Smith, the renowned Columbia University historian, claimed to have discovered a new "secret" Gospel of Mark. The text he uncovered included a segment where Jesus spent the night with a rich young man to teach him the mysteries of the kingdom of God. Smith strongly hinted that this "baptism" ceremony contained a homosexual component. This new "secret" part of the book of Mark gave him the opportunity to advance his pet theory that Jesus was merely an ancient magician. The only problem was that his discovery turned out to be a forgery, and it is almost certain that Smith forged it himself. There are numerous clues that support this conclusion: problems in the formation of the letters and the consistency of the lines in the handwriting, anachronistic elements in the text, and even "too clever by half" clues revealing his own identity. Perhaps most damning was a problem that plagues most literary forgeries: It reflected the perspective of its milieu—in this case the 1950s and 1960s—rather than the period it purported to be from. To Morton Smith it was a brilliant joke that played off his own sexuality. It worked. The book he published in 1973 is still in print even though most serious scholars now dismiss it. On another level *The Secret Gospel of Mark* is quintessentially post-modern. Even a forgery can be authentic if it reflects the strongly held beliefs of the forger. Moreover, as one scholar observes, he used the jargon of textual criticism to obscure the contradictions and mistruths in his argument.

There's a more recent example of this danger. Karen King, a well-respected scholar, announced at a conference in Rome in 2012 that she had discovered a fragment of an early Christian Coptic text from Egypt that strongly suggested that Jesus had a wife. King held the Hollis Professorship at Harvard Divinity School, the oldest endowed divinity chair in the United States. The highly provocative nature of the discovery ensured that it would be front page news. It appeared in the *New York Times* and *Washington Post*. The only problem was that it became apparent over the next few years that her discovery was based on a hoax. Ariel Sabar brilliantly exposed the fraud in a magazine article in *The Atlantic* that he expanded into his recently published, critically acclaimed book *Veritas*. Some perceptive scholars caught on to it immediately, but they didn't have the institutional prestige that King possessed. Sabar traced the provenance of the forgery and found that the man who provided her with the fragment was a master manipulator. He studied Egyptology briefly at the Free University of Berlin but later made his livelihood in many, mostly questionable, ways, including running a porn site on the internet. Sabar also learned that the technical experts that King utilized to confirm the fragment's authenticity had either family or personal connections to her. The whole affair underlines how a post-modern mindset allowed King to be duped by a sociopathic con man. History to her was not about facts but rather gender, its objective to enrich our imagination, the goal not to understand the past but rather reflect the present. King viewed the orthodox cannon as oppressive and misogynistic and was attracted to the gnostic texts instead. She fell for the forgery against her better judgment because it showed what she wanted to see. In fact, when the proof became overwhelming that it was all a hoax, King's response was not remorse but rather exasperation. The controversy about forgery, she said, was taking away from the validity of her argument. In short, it was all about her.

Morton Smith knowingly perpetuated a hoax. Karen King was the unwitting victim of one because of her preconceived notions. Both events, however, have one thing in common. They show what can happen when modern perspectives are imposed on the Bible. However, a literal interpretation of the Bible is not the answer. If we believe everything literally, how do we handle the many contradictions and discrepancies in the text? Ignore them. Compartmentalize them. Lamely explain them away. To an historian none of these approaches are options. Sensible biblical criticism is not only a necessity; it also enriches our understanding of the text. Biblical critics need to be grounded in both the text itself and its historical context, rejecting any temptation to impose their own viewpoints.

By establishing the indispensability of eyewitness testimony, Bauckham and his colleagues reground the Gospels, making them profoundly real. By understanding that they are on one level historical texts, we can deal with the inconsistencies and come closer to the truth. The witnesses were real people who saw real things. The writers of the Gospels were human despite their divine inspiration. What they saw and heard was processed through the mentality of the first century. In order to better understand the Gospels, we need to view them through the lens of history. If Jesus came to earth today, he'd be the same living God, but we would tell the story very differently from our ancestors.

Some biblical scholars, who had initially trained for the ministry— and this includes Morton Smith—rejected their faith because of the contradictions imbedded in the Gospels. Superficially this is not an irrational response, but there's another more constructive one. Christians believe the Gospels are divinely inspired. It's why we believe the Bible is the word of God. However, even if they are inspired by God, humans are still human. Everyone will view what they see and hear from their perspective, shaped by their own life and experience. It's natural that they'll see the same things in slightly different ways. Indeed, it would be much more suspicious if there were no internal contradictions. This is one reason why the early church fathers chose to accept all four Gospels rather than choose one. Why have four Gospels if there was one authoritative account? Simple. The very human imperfections and contradictions reinforce their authenticity.

Jesus's world was rich in diversity, often paradoxical, and one of extremes. Rural poverty and landlessness plagued the countryside, but

Jerusalem was one of the richest cities in the Roman Empire, its temple a major religious shrine and ancient tourist attraction. Jews set themselves apart, following the law, but Judea, Galilee, and their environs also had a large gentile population. Jesus spoke Aramaic and most likely read Hebrew, but like many Jews could communicate in Greek. Even among his own people, diversity ruled. However, all Jews revered the temple and the Torah. The Torah was their constitution, defining them as a distinct nation unlike any other in the Roman Empire, one that despite all its internal feuds had the confidence to stand up to Rome. By looking at the revolt closely, not under the spell of Josephus, it becomes clear that it was not a random, tragic sequence of events. Rather it was controlled by men, including those in the highest strata of the elite, who perceived themselves as a nation that could stand separate from Rome. They really thought they could pull it off. Only our modern perspective makes defeat look inevitable.

Even Judaism itself was not uniform. The Sadducees held firmly to traditional beliefs, based on temple and Torah, but the Essenes and the Pharisees believed more, especially concerning the afterlife. In a world of chaos and evil, myth also played a vital role. The common people believed in magic, demons, and occasionally the old gods. Jesus was a part of this rich tableaux.

I believe that a deeper knowledge of this world provides the reader with a greater understanding of the Gospels, providing context and perspective, which in turn enhances our understanding. When Mark, for example, describes the Herodians, Pharisees, and scribes challenging Jesus, it's important to know exactly who he's talking about. Otherwise, they appear merely as cardboard straight men. Moreover, knowledge of the history and the society teaches us about the Bible itself: why and how it was written, its survival, its relevance. Literacy, oral tradition, and the mixture of the two all played a critical role. Roman roads, sea lanes, and above all peace, the Pax Romana, allowed the Gospels to spread throughout the empire. The fact that the Gospels were written in Greek universalized the message, which traveled on the information network of the day, the "holy internet." The oral and literary traditions melded together and reinforced each other. The story the Gospels told were ancient biographies about a real person and based on the hard evidence of eyewitness observers, the criteria necessary to be selected as the official cannon by the church fathers. No doubt the theology implicit in many of the gnostic Gospels was highly suspect to the early church fathers, but selection was not based on warring theologies.

It was grounded on how close the authors of them were to the teachings of Jesus and the traditions preserved by his disciples. The church fathers valued the testimony provided by eyewitnesses. Although it's very difficult, if not impossible, to bring to life the "historical," as opposed to spiritual, Jesus, we can provide a nuanced picture of the historical world around him. This is no small thing.

Finding the "historical" Jesus is a fool's errand, but understanding his world is an attainable goal. We can't understand the New Testament without a knowledge of the perspective of the writers who created the Gospels. Without historical context their meaning is impossible to comprehend. The Gospels without a knowledge of the history behind them is like a Shakespeare play performed in modern dress. Sure, it keeps the rich language, the profound insights into the human condition, but at its heart it seems a little silly and inauthentic. Yes, Shakespeare represents the universal, but he was still a man firmly grounded in his time. If we don't understand this, we'll either miss or misperceive what he's saying. It's the same with the Bible. Its relevance is not derived from reading into it everything that we want. Rather it is profound when the texts are grounded on a firm historical foundation. Moreover, an understanding of the genre of the Gospels is vital. By knowing what they are, that is, ancient biography, our confidence in them is much greater than if we perceive them to be the product of undisciplined oral transmission. And if we add to that the knowledge that ancient biographers based their work on the testimony of reliable eyewitnesses, our confidence is further increased. We have four Gospels telling the story of the Savior. How can that not be anything but relevant?

My journey to learn about the world that Jesus lived in provided an answer to a question that had always haunted me. How did a small Jewish sect become the official religion of the Roman Empire within a few short centuries? I asked a pastor I highly respect this question a few years ago. In his eyes the answer was obvious. In fact, he even seemed surprised by the question itself. God simply meant it to be. On a theological level this might suffice, but as a historian I wanted more, not necessarily to contradict his answer but to enhance it. Let's look at the world of Jesus. It was, as we have observed, "a world full of gods." People were craving something, whether it was meaning in their lives or the hope of eternal life. They searched for spiritual sustenance in many places: magic, mystery cults, philosophy, even the old local gods and goddesses. The fact that they saw no contradiction in seeking answers from different sources simultaneously shows that they were not completely satisfied with any one of them. Judaism was unique. It provided its followers, through the law, precise guidelines on how to live. At the same, time Judaism also allowed its mythological, apocalyptic strand to explain the unexplainable, not only providing answers to the problem of the existence of evil but also giving hope of life after death. Initially there was no clear separation between Christianity and Judaism. Then, tragically, the cradle of both faiths was torn asunder. The failure of the great revolt against Rome led to the destruction of the temple and, by decimation of the temple cult, the foundation of traditional Judaism. Judaism would survive and flourish under the rabbis. Even such a great loss could not destroy it, a true sign of strength. However, the followers of Jesus were now fundamentally separated from Judaism, a new, separate identity guaranteed. The Gospels were written. The "holy internet" provided a means for it to spread across the Mediterranean world, the Roman peace ensuring this. The persecutor was also the protector. The new faith was uniquely prepared. The world in which Jesus lived, ancient Palestine, was a diverse one. Jews and gentiles lived in proximity in a multilingual environment. Judaism and Hellenism coexisted. Despite the tensions that finally exploded into revolt against Rome, it was a cosmopolitan society almost despite itself. It was just the fertile ground for a new faith to develop that would also appeal to the world outside of it.

Religious thinkers have grappled with the tension between history and theology for centuries, seeing them as mutually exclusive. Even the most liberal theologians, while not rejecting history, segregate it to its own realm. My belief is that this tension does not exist. The study of history only enhances our understanding of the Gospels. Viewing them through history's lens can only serve to strengthen our faith.

Bibliographical Essay

WHEN I WROTE MY dissertation years ago, I had a simple rule for including a book: if cracked open once, it's included. I'm not going to take that approach here. Books are cited for two reasons: First, to give credit to those scholars who provided me with key facts and provocative ideas. Second, to present the reader with the best books to pursue the topics I've touched on here. These recommendations are not meant to be a complete and balanced guide to the field. Rather they're more like a road map of my own education. All the books I've used are listed in my bibliography. The most important ones are discussed in this essay. Please refer to the full bibliography for the complete citations.

Aside from the Four Gospels, the most important source for Jesus's world is the works of Josephus. His complete works, including *Jewish Antiquities* and *The Jewish War* can be found in *The New Complete Works of Josephus*. There is a new translation by Martin Hammond of *The Jewish War* that is probably the best place to start for the curious reader. An introduction and notes by the esteemed historian Martin Goodman is an added premium. The *Carta's Illustrated the Jewish Civil War* provides numerous illustrations, maps, and family trees.

Josephus is an eyewitness to many of the events in the revolt against Rome. While this adds immeasurably to the vividness of his account, Josephus's divided loyalties and personal agenda are problematic for the historian. Martin Goodman provides a succinct overview of the "Josephus problem" in his *Josephus's The Jewish War: A Biography*. Tessa Rajak in *Josephus* also provides valuable context. For a more academic perspective consult *Flavius Josephus and Flavian Rome*, a collection of essays, and Steve Mason's *Josephus, Judea, and Christian Origins*. James S. McLaren takes a more revisionist approach in *Turbulent Times?*, arguing that scholars must move beyond the framework built by Josephus when using the text as a source.

The standard scholarly treatment of Palestine at the time of Jesus, Emil Schürer's monumental *A History of the Jewish People in the Time of Jesus Christ*, was published over a century ago in Germany. Although a valuable research tool, it's now out of date. A book well worth reading is Martin Goodman's *Rome and Jerusalem*. It provides an overview of the period from the perspective of the tension between these two peoples. *The Jews under Roman Rule* by Mary Smallwood furnishes a comprehensive history not only in Palestine but also in the rest of the Mediterranean. Steve Mason's erudite *Orientation to the History of Roman Judaea* is also useful, but it's aimed at an academic audience.

An invaluable reference work is *The Anchor Bible Dictionary*, six volumes long and packed full of information. The three volume *Encyclopedia of Ancient Christianity* is also helpful, as is *The Oxford Dictionary of the Christian Church*.

Herod the Great and his family are not treated sympathetically in the Gospels, and that's putting it mildly. Nevertheless, this deeply flawed but remarkable man did more to create Jesus's world than any other individual. There are several fascinating books that trace his career and enumerate his achievements. The primary source for Herod, not surprisingly, is Josephus. Perhaps the best introduction to this fascinating character is *The Herods of Judaea* by A. H. M. Jones. Unfortunately, this clear and concise work by the renowned Cambridge historian of Rome is out of print. Géza Vermes's more recent *The True Herod*, with excellent illustration and color maps, is short and engaging. Both Samuel Rocca's *Herod's Judea* and Adam Kolman Marshak's *The Many Faces of Herod the Great* are well-written academic studies. Rocca is particularly interesting in his discussion of Herod's court and the rebuilding of the temple. Marshak is particularly insightful on the balancing act that Herod was required to perform: Roman client, Hellenistic monarch, and Jewish king. Both *Herod the Great* by Norman Gelb and *The Herods* by Bruce Chilton are aimed at a popular audience, emphasizing the murder and mayhem in his dysfunctional family. Nikos Kokkinos, in his *The Herodian Dynasty*, focuses on the origins of the dynasty and provides a detailed account of Herod's progeny. Harold W. Hoehner's *Herod Antipas* is an interesting account of King Herod's son who ruled Galilee and Perea at the time of Jesus. He is best known for his execution of John the Baptist.

The Jewish revolt against Rome occurred a generation after the death of Jesus, but it had a profound influence on Judaism, Christianity, and the creation of the Gospels. The narrative provided by Josephus is unrivaled, but there are a few books among the massive literature on the subject that I found particularly helpful. Martin Goodman's indispensable *The Ruling Class of Judaea* is in a class of its own. Not only does he expertly delineate the social tensions that bred revolt, but Goodman provides the best introduction to the society of first-century Judea and Galilee. Michael Owen Wise focuses on the high priest Ananias and his family in a fascinating essay in *Thunder in Gemini*. He argues persuasively that this elite priestly family fully supported the rebellion. For a modern history of the revolt nothing surpasses Steve Mason's detailed and informative *A History of the Jewish War*. For the destruction of Jerusalem, see *The Roman Siege of Jerusalem* by Rupert Furneaux.

As mentioned above, Goodman's book on the Judean ruling class is essential reading for understanding Jewish society at the time of Jesus, but, although it describes a later period, his *State and Society in Roman Galilee* is also very useful. *The Oxford Handbook of Jewish Daily Life in Roman Palestine* is essential for understanding the daily life at that time. The essays by eminent scholars are highly informative and accessible to the general reader. Two fine monographs describe and analyze the Babatha archives, which preserved valuable information about Jewish society, law, literacy, and the role of women. These are Kimberley Czajkowski's *Localized Law* and Philip. F. Esler's *Babatha's Orchard*. Michael L. Satlow's *Jewish Marriage in Antiquity* is also worth consulting. For the role of scribes in Jewish society see Christine Schams's *Jewish Scribes in the Second-Temple Period*. Lee I. Levine provides an excellent overview of Jerusalem's role in the society and economy in his *Jerusalem* while Joachim Jeremias gives a more detailed account in his *Jerusalem in the Time of Jesus*.

Keith Hopkins in his *A World Full of Gods* brilliantly captures the religious ethos of the Roman world at the time of Christ. The supernatural permeated people's lives, pushing them to find meaning outside the established civic religions. *Ancient Mystery Cults*, by Walter Burkert, is a succinct introduction to this search for theological meaning. As for Judaism, its development from a syncretic faith to a monotheistic religion is much more complex than most of us believe. This rich complexity is captured in Richard Elliot Friedman's engrossing *Who Wrote the Bible?* His analysis brings together the various strands of Judaism culminating in the

Hebrew scriptures that we know today. However, the faith that emerged prior to the time of Jesus, based on the law and the temple, did not meet the needs of people searching for deeper spiritual meaning. Therefore, as Seth Schwartz argues in his *Imperialism and Jewish Society*, an apocalyptic tradition emerged, coexisting with the official religion. It turned to myth in order to deal with such issues as the existence of evil and the possibility of an afterlife, further enriching Judaism.

Josephus set the parameters for discussing the various Jewish sects, each reflecting strands of the rich religious environment, but his analysis is aimed at a gentile audience and downplays the richness and complexity of his subject. Modern scholars have rectified the situation. Albert I. Baumgartner's *The Flourishing of Jewish Sects in the Maccabean Era: An Interpretation* is valuable. Two books of essays, *The Pharisees* and *In Quest of the Historical Pharisees*, frame the current academic debate about the Pharisees. As far as the Dead Sea Scrolls are concerned, Norman Golb provides an introduction in his innovative and provocative *Who Wrote the Dead Sea Scrolls?* A new translation of the Dead Sea Scrolls, by Michael Wise, Martin Abegg Jr. and Edward Cook, also provides useful context.

John Barton's *A History of the Bible* is perhaps the best introduction to both the Old and New Testaments. His *The Nature of Biblical Criticism* clearly delineates the issues surrounding this often-fraught subject. Of all the books I've read in my research, Richard Bauckham's *Jesus and the Eyewitnesses* was the most eye opening. Not only does his book turn the whole field of biblical criticism upside down, but it also adds a profound measure of authenticity to the Gospels themselves. He has contributed many articles and reviews to the dialogue, and many of these are collected in his *The Jewish World around the New Testament* and *The Christian World around the New Testament*. Bauckham has also edited *The Gospels for All Christians* that contains a few provocative essays. These include his discussion of the Gospel's original audience, Richard Burridge's essay on the genre of the gospels, Loveday Alexander's essay on ancient book production, and Michael B. Thompson's groundbreaking analysis of the "holy internet."

Over thirty years ago, William V. Harris set the terms for the debate of literacy in the classical world in his *Ancient Literacy*. Although his broad thesis gained acceptance quickly, Harris's monograph elicited a flurry of academic research on the topic. Within two years *Literacy in the Ancient World* was published. It contains articles by eminent scholars including Mary Beard, Keith Hopkins, and Alan K. Bowman that are relevant to this study. Shortly thereafter, Bowman and Greg Wolf edited *Literacy and Power in the Ancient World*, which contains an essay by Martin Goodman on the power of scribes in Roman Judea. Finally, Michael Owen Wise used the Bar Kokhba archives for his definitive *Language and Literacy in Roman Judaea*.

Any discussion of the oral tradition needs to start with Milman Parry, the Indiana Jones of classical studies. During the early 1930s, he observed and recorded the local bards of the former Yugoslavia, who recited traditional sagas, and used his finding to analyze the role of oral transmission in the creation of the Homeric epics. His findings were published after his early, tragic death by his former student, Albert B. Lord, in *The Singer of Tales*. The *Making of Homeric Verse* is a collection of his articles, reviews, and unpublished manuscripts compiled by his son, Adam Parry. A fascinating biography of Parry, *Hearing Homer's Song* by Robert Kanigel, has recently been published.

Kenneth E. Bailey utilized his anthropological observations of modern Arab village storytelling to develop valuable insights into the role of orality in the formation of the Gospels in *Poet and Peasant* and *Through Peasant Eyes*. His seminal article "Informal Controlled Oral Tradition and the Synoptic Gospels" helped define the parameters of the academic dialogue. Samuel Byrskog's *Story as History—History as Story* uses the rabbinic tradition to cast more light on oral tradition. Both scholars buttress Bauckham's argument that the early oral renderings of Jesus's teachings were transmitted by reliable eyewitnesses and not corrupted in the transmission.

Forgeries and literary hoaxes have a long and fascinating history. The eminent intellectual historian Anthony Grafton puts the issue into context in his *Forgers and Critics*. When scholars allow their beliefs and prejudices to cloud their research, the results can be disastrous. Karen King is a case in point. The Hollis Professor of Divinity at Harvard University and the author of well-respected books, including *What Is Gnosticism?*, was the victim of a literary hoax by a notorious con man. King publicly announced that a newly discovered Coptic fragment indicated that Jesus was married. To make matters worse, the whole sordid affair was uncovered by the respected journalist Ariel Sabar, who published a brilliant expose in his *Veritas: A Harvard Professor, a Con Man, and the Gospel of Jesus's Wife*. If King was the unwitting victim of a nefarious hoax, Morton Smith, the eminent Columbia historian, was the perpetrator of one. When *The Secret Gospel of Mark* was published fifty years ago, it was an academic sensation that shook up biblical research at its very foundations. Although controversial from the start, it received enthusiastic reviews, including one from the eminent historian Hugh Trevor-Roper. Elaine Pagels, the respected Princeton historian of religion and author of the classic *The Gnostic Gospels*, wrote a respectful foreword for the book. Two recent works, the first by a lawyer and the second by a respected academic, prove that Smith's seminal work was almost certainly a hoax based on a nonexistent source. These books are *The Gospel Hoax* by Stephen C. Carlson and *The Secret Gospel of Mark Unveiled* by Peter Jeffery.

Bibliography

Bailey, Kenneth E. "Informal Controlled Oral Tradition and the Synoptic Gospels." *Asia Journal of Theology* 5 (1991) 34–51.

—. *Poet & Peasant; and, Through Peasant Eyes: A Literary-Cultural Approach to the Parables in Luke.* Grand Rapids, MI: Eerdmans, 1999.

Barton, John. *A History of the Bible.* New York: Viking, 2019.

—. *The Nature of Biblical Criticism.* Louisville and London: Westminster John Knox, 2007.

Bauckham, Richard. *The Christian World around the New Testament.* Grand Rapids, MI: Baker Academic, 2017.

—, ed. *The Gospels for All Christians: Rethinking the Gospel Audiences.* Grand Rapids, MI: Eerdmans, 2004.

—. *Jesus and the Eyewitnesses: The Gospels as Eyewitness Testimony.* Grand Rapids, MI: Eerdmans, 2017.

—. *The Jewish World around the New Testament.* Grand Rapids, MI: Baker Academic, 2010.

Baumgartner, Albert I. *The Flourishing of Jewish Sects in the Maccabean Era: An Interpretation.* Leiden: Brill, 1997.

Beck, Roger. *The Religion of the Mithras Cult in the Roman Empire.* Oxford: Oxford University Press, 2006.

Bird, Michael. *The Gospel of the Lord: How the Early Church Wrote the Story of Jesus.* Grand Rapids, MI: Eerdmans, 2014.

Bowman, Alan K., and Greg Woolf, eds. *Literacy and Power in the Ancient World.* Cambridge: Cambridge University Press, 1994.

Burkert, Walter. *Ancient Mystery Cults.* Cambridge, MA: Harvard University Press, 1987.

Byrskog, Samuel. *Story as History—History as Story: The Gospel Tradition in the Context of Ancient Oral History.* Tübingen: Mohr Siebeck, 2000.

Carlson, Stephen C. *The Gospel Hoax: Morton Smith's Invention of Secret Mark.* Waco, TX: Baylor University Press, 2005.

Chilton, Bruce. *The Herods: Murder, Politics, and the Art of Succession.* Minneapolis: Fortress, 2021.

Clauss, Manfred. *The Roman Cult of Mithras: The God and His Mysteries.* New York: Routledge, 1990.

The Complete Apocrypha: With Enoch, Jasher, and Jubilees. Monee, IL: Covenant, 2019.

Cross, F. L., and E. A. Livingstone, eds. *The Oxford Dictionary of the Christian Church.* Oxford: Oxford University Press, 1997.

Czajkowski, Kimberly. *Localized Law: The Babatha and Salome Komaise Archives.* Oxford: Oxford University Press, 2017.

Di Benardino, ed. *Encyclopedia of Ancient Christianity*. 3 vols. Westmont, IL: InterVarsity, 1999–2014.

———. *Encyclopedia of the Early Church*. 2 vols. New York: Oxford University Press, 1992.

Dunn, James D. G. *Jesus Remembered: Christianity in the Making*. Grand Rapids, MI: Eerdmans, 2003.

Edmonson, Jonathan, et al., eds. *Flavius Josephus and Flavian Rome*. Oxford: Oxford University Press, 2005.

Ehrman, Bart D. *The New Testament: An Early Christian Introduction to the Early Christian Writings*. New York: Oxford University Press, 1997.

Esler, Philip Francis. *Babatha's Orchard: The Yadin Papyri and an Ancient Jewish Family Tale Retold*. Oxford: Oxford University Press, 2017.

Freedman, David Noel, ed. *The Anchor Bible Dictionary*. Garden City, NY: Doubleday, 1964.

Friedman, Richard Elliot. *The Bible with Sources Revealed: A New View of the Five Books of Moses*. New York: HarperOne, 2003.

———. *Who Wrote the Bible?* New York: Simon & Schuster, 1997.

Furneaux, Rupert. *The Roman Siege of Jerusalem*. London: Davis MacGibbon, 1973.

Gelb, Norman. *Herod the Great: Statesman, Visionary, Tyrant*. Lanham, MD: Rowman & Littlefield, 2013.

Golb, Norman. *Who Wrote the Dead Sea Scrolls? The Search for the Secret of Qumran*. New York: Scribner, 1995.

Goodman, Martin. *Josephus's The Jewish War: A Biography*. Princeton: Princeton University Press, 2019.

———. *Rome and Jerusalem: A Clash of Ancient Civilizations*. New York: Vintage, 2008.

———. *The Ruling Class of Judaea: The Origins of the Jewish Revolt against Rome A.D. 66–70*. Cambridge: Cambridge University Press, 1987.

———. *State and Society in Roman Galilee, AD 132–212*. London and Portland, OR: Valentine Mitchell, 1983.

Grafton, Anthony, and Ann Blair. *Forgers and Critics: Creativity and Duplicity in Western Scholarship*. Princeton: Princeton University Press, 2019.

Harris, William V. *Ancient Literacy*. Cambridge, MA: Harvard University Press, 1984.

———. *Rome's Imperial Economy: Twelve Essays*. Oxford: Oxford University Press, 2011.

Hennecke, Edgar, and Wilhelm Schneemelcher. *New Testament Apocrypha*. Cambridge: Clarke, 1991.

Hezser, Catherine, ed. *The Oxford Handbook of Jewish Daily Life in Roman Palestine*. Oxford: Oxford University Press, 2010.

Hoehner, Harold W. *Herod Antipas: A Contemporary of Jesus Christ*. Grand Rapids, MI: Zondervan, 1980.

Hopkins, Keith. *A World Full of Gods: The Strange Triumph of Christianity*. New York: Penguin, 1999.

Humphrey, J. H., ed. "Literacy in the Ancient World." *Journal of Roman Archeology* Supplementary Series 3. Ann Arbor, MI: 1991.

Jeffery, Peter. *The Secret Gospel of Mark Unveiled: Imagined Rituals of Sex, Death, and Madness in a Biblical Forgery*. New Haven: Yale University Press, 2007.

Jeremias, Joachim. *Jerusalem in the Time of Jesus*. Minneapolis: Fortress, 1969.

Jones, A. H. M. *Cities of the Eastern Roman Empire*. Oxford: Oxford University Press, 1937.

————. *The Herods of Judaea.* Oxford: Clarendon, 1967.

Josephus, Flavius. *Josephus: Carta's Illustrated the Jewish War.* Jerusalem: Carta Jerusalem, 2016.

————. *The New Complete Works of Josephus.* Grand Rapids, MI: Kregel, 1999.

————. *The Jewish War.* Oxford: Oxford University Press, 2017.

Kanigel, Robert. *Hearings Homer's Song: The Brief Life and Big Idea of Milman Parry.* New York: Knopf, 2021.

King, Karen L. *What Is Gnosticism?* Cambridge, MA: Belknap, 2003.

Kokkinos, Nikos. *The Herodian Dynasty.* London: SPINK, 2010.

Levine, Lee I. *Jerusalem: Portrait of the City in the Second Temple Period (538 B.C.E.-70 C.E.).* Philadelphia: Jewish Publication Society, 2002.

Lord, Albert B. *The Singer of Tales.* Cambridge, MA: Harvard University Press, 2019.

Marshak, Adam Kolman. *The Many Faces of Herod the Great.* Grand Rapids, MI: Eerdmans, 2015.

Mason, Steve. *A History of the Jewish War, A.D. 66-74.* Cambridge: Cambridge University Press, 2016.

————. *Josephus, Judea, and Christian Origins: Methods and Categories.* Peabody, MA: Hendrickson, 2009.

————. *Orientation to the History of Roman Judaea.* Eugene, OR: Cascade, 2016.

McLaren, James S. *Turbulent Times? Josephus and Scholarship on Judaea in the First Century CE.* Sheffield: Sheffield Academic, 1998.

Meyer, Marvin. *The Nag Hammadi Scriptures.* New York: HarperOne, 2007.

Neusner, Jacob, and Bruce Chilton, eds. *In Quest of the Historical Pharisees.* Waco, TX: Baylor University Press, 2007.

Pagels, Elaine. *Beyond Belief: The Secret Gospel of Thomas.* New York: Random House, 2003.

————. *The Gnostic Gospels.* New York: Vintage, 1979.

Parry, Adam, ed. *The Making of Homeric Verse: The Collected Papers of Milman Parry.* Oxford: Oxford University Press, 1987.

Pliny the Elder. *The Historie of the World, Commonly Called the Naturall Historie of C. Plinius Secundus.* London: Adam Islip, 1601.

Rajak, Tessa. *Josephus.* London: Bristol Classical, 2002.

Reece, Steve. "The Myth of Milman Parry: Ajax or Elpenor." *Oral Tradition* (2019) 115-42.

Rocca, Samuel. *Herod's Judea: A Mediterranean State in the Classical World.* Eugene, OR: Wipf & Stock, 2008.

Rocca, Samuel, and Christa Hook. *The Army of Herod the Great.* Oxford: Osprey, 2009.

Rogers, Cleon L. *The Topical Josephus.* Grand Rapids, MI: Zondervan, 1992.

Roller, Duane W. *A Historical and Topographical Guide to the Geography of Strabo.* Cambridge: Cambridge University Press, 2018.

Sabar, Ariel. *Veritas: A Harvard Professor, a Con Man, and the Gospel of Jesus's Wife.* New York: Doubleday, 2020.

Sanders, E. P. *Jesus and Judaism.* Philadelphia: Fortress, 1985.

Satlow, Michael L. *Jewish Marriage in Antiquity.* Princeton: Princeton University Press, 2001.

Schams, Christine. *Jewish Scribes in the Second-Temple Period.* Sheffield: Sheffield Academic, 1998.

Scholem, Gershom. *The Messianic Idea in Judaism and Other Essays on Jewish Spirituality.* New York: Schocken, 1995.

Schwartz, Seth. *Imperialism and Jewish Society: 200 B.C.E. to 640 C.E.* Princeton: Princeton University Press, 2001.

Schürer, Emil. *A History of the Jewish People in the Time of Jesus Christ.* Peabody, MA: Hendrickson, 2018.

Sievers, Joseph, and Amy-Jill Levine. *The Pharisees.* Grand Rapids, MI: Eerdmans, 2021.

Smallwood, E. Mary. *The Jews under Roman Rule: From Pompey to Diocletian: A Study in Political Relations.* Atlanta: SBL, 2015.

Smith, Morton. *Clement of Alexandria and a Secret Gospel of Mark.* Cambridge, MA: Harvard University Press, 1973.

———. *Jesus the Magician.* New York: HarperCollins, 1981.

———. *Palestinian Parties and Politics That Shaped the Old Testament.* New York: Columbia University Press, 1971.

———. *The Secret Gospel: The Discovery and Interpretation of the Secret Gospel According to Mark.* Middletown, CA: Dawn Horse, 2005.

Smith, Morton, and Shaye J. D. Cohen, eds. *Studies in the Cult of Yahweh.* Leiden: Brill Academic, 1996.

Theissen, Gerd. *The Gospels in Context: Social and Political History in the Synoptic Tradition.* Edinburgh: Clark International, 1992.

Trevor-Roper, Hugh. "'Gospel of Liberty.'" *Sunday Times,* Jun 30, 1974.

Turcan, Robert. *The Cults of the Roman Empire.* Hoboken, NJ: Wiley-Blackwell, 1997.

Vermes Géza. *The Complete Dead Sea Scrolls.* New York: Penguin, 1961.

———. *The True Herod.* London: Bloomsbury T. & T. Clark, 2014.

Werblowsky, R. J. Zwi and Geoffrey Wigoder, eds. *The Oxford History of the Jewish Religion.* Oxford: Oxford University Press, 1997.

Wise, Michael Owen. *Language and Literacy in Roman Judaea: A Study of the Bas Kokhba Documents.* New Haven: Yale University Press, 2015.

———. "The Life and Times of Ananias bar Nedebaeus and His Family." In *Thunder in Gemini and Other Essays on the History, Language, and Literature of Second Temple Palestine,* 51–102. Sheffield: Sheffield Academic, 1994.

Wise, Michael Owen, et al., trans. *The Dead Sea Scrolls.* New York: HarperOne, 1996, 2005.

Wilson, A. N. *The Book of the People: How to Read the Bible.* London: Atlantic, 2015.

Younge, C. D. *The Works of Philo.* Peabody, MA: Hendrickson, 2018.

Index